TRAINING TALK

conversations
with a dozen
master coaches

TRAINING TALK

conversations with a dozen master coaches

G. MARTIN BINGISSER

Published by HMMR Media LLC
HMMR Media LLC
4230 137th Avenue NE
Bellevue, WA 98005
www.hmmrmedia.com

Copyright © 2018 by Glen Martin Bingisser

All rights reserved. This book or any portion thereof may not be reproduced or used in any form without prior written consent from the publisher.

First published, 2018
ISBN: 978-0-9915361-1-5

Printed in the United States of America
10 9 8 7 6 5 4 3 2 1
Set in Minion Pro

List of Illustrations
Cover photo by Chris Karidis on Unsplash (*www.unsplash.com*)
(9) Vern Gambetta at the 2018 Gain Conference, courtesy of author; (21) Harry Marra, courtesy of Harry Marra; (33) Dan Pfaff, courtesy of Dan Pfaff; (82) Anatoliy Bondarchuk coaching at a 2014 training camp in Sweden, courtesy of author; (128) Tom Myslinski courtesy of Tom Myslinski; (143) Frans Bosch consulting with Japan Rugby, courtesy of Frans Bosch; (157) John Pryor working with Fiji Rugby, courtesy of John Pryor; (169) John Kiely working with Irish Rugby, courtesy of John Kiely

*for Kate, who wears many hats . . .
wife, mother, lawyer, editor, designer, project manager, and fan*

CONTENTS

Foreword ix
Introduction xiii

PART I // AT THE TRACK 1
   1 // Vern Gambetta 7
   2 // Harry Marra 19
   3 // Dan Pfaff 31
   4 // Gary Winckler 51
   5 // Pat Connolly 67
   6 // Anatoliy Bondarchuk 79
   7 // Derek Evely 89

PART II // ON THE FIELD 111
   8 // Dave Tenney 115
   9 // Tom Myslinski 127
   10 // Frans Bosch 141
   11 // John Pryor 155
   12 // John Kiely 167

Afterword 201
Acknowledgements 205
About the Author 207

FOREWORD

Back in 1987, I took a leap of faith. After 20 years of experience as a track and field coach, I moved to a new town for a new job in a new sport as director of conditioning for the Chicago White Sox. I was confident I could handle the challenge, but in the back of my mind there was still some doubt. I had never worked in baseball before, and the profession I had entered, athletic development, hadn't even existed a few years prior.

After arriving, the doubt quickly faded as I took a look at baseball through the eyes of a track coach. Why didn't my javelin throwers have the shoulder problems that pitchers did? It was simple: I started looking at the pitchers as javelin throwers in long pants. I took what I knew about preparing the whole kinetic chain to throw the javelin far and adapted that to the demands of pitching. To the surprise of many, we stopped having shoulder problems, and the pitchers became more durable. This was a lesson I was then able to apply many times over in other sports. Don't look at the sport as a unique activity, instead look at the movements, and connect that to what is being done in other sports. This is a lesson you will learn from the coaches in this book. If they have one commonality, it is the ability to see movement with different eyes and make adjustments accordingly.

No matter the sport, a good coaching philosophy must stay true to the same fundamental truths of coaching. In this book, Martin has sought to discover

TRAINING TALK

these truths through interviews with some of the best minds in coaching today. This book is a reflection of Martin's intellectual curiosity and passion to learn. His probing questions allow you, the reader, to get to the essence of the concepts and training methods.

I am honored and humbled to write this Foreword and to be included as one of the coaches interviewed for this collection. These coaches are an eclectic mix of experts from athletics and field sports, but the one thing they have in common is that they are the best of the best. Together, the interviews provide a comprehensive overview of the process of developing the athlete from many points of view. Most importantly, as I did 30 years ago, each of these coaches has gone outside their specialty and, in many instances outside their sport, to learn and challenge themselves to improve. This sends a powerful message about what it takes to be on the cutting edge.

By selecting coaches that transcend sports and disciplines, Martin underscores the unity of training ideas and concepts. The need to communicate across sports to share knowledge and learn. This collection of interviews features coaches who are thought leaders that have produced results at the highest levels of sport using this approach. None of them is narrow in their areas of interest or specialization. They all go where they need to go to find answers. They all use lateral thinking to connect dots in seemingly unrelated manners. They did this, not by being followers, but by questioning and building connections outside their fields of expertise.

All of these coaches share:
- deep knowledge;
- passion that fuels their drive to learn;
- coaching the athlete, not the sport or event;
- achievement at the highest levels;
- continued learning; and
- strength in getting better at getting better.

Foreword

Reflect on the ideas expressed here and each of these approaches. Think critically about the responses. Do not take any of the answers as gospel. Use the collective wisdom of these coaches to learn and grow. It may change your ideas, or it may confirm them. Regardless, the benefit will be improved coaching. Keep learning!

VERN GAMBETTA

INTRODUCTION

I AM THE first person to tell a coach <u>not to copy others</u>. Every athlete is different, and training should be designed to fit the individual. On the other hand, if you notice something that every top coach is doing, you would be foolish not to include it in your own programming. These commonalities are what I am after when I sit down with the world's top coaches. I like to learn about their training methods, processes, and philosophy, and most importantly, see what they all have in common. In this way, I can better understand the truly successful part of each program.

I started HMMR Media as a public forum to work through my own coach's training methods. I wanted to see why we did what we did, and doing so online allowed for input from around the world that helped me learn more in the process. What I didn't know when I started the site was that the bigger benefit would be the access it has given me to some of the world's best coaches. I've been able to sit down with coaches of world record holders, Olympic champions, and leading sports scientists.

In this book, I've compiled talks I've had with a dozen of the world's leading coaches around the theme of training methods. The coaches come from a variety of backgrounds and a variety of sports. What the interviews have in common is that they focus on lessons that can be learned from and implemented by any coach.

TRAINING TALK

This book is divided into two parts. Part I includes interviews with coaches that come from the world of track and field. As a track and field coach myself, this is my family, and since track and field contains the basic elements of sport—running, jumping, and throwing—it is a great platform from which to learn.

Part II moves on to talk about training methods with some leading physical preparation coaches from field sports. Field, court, and team sports have their own special dynamics: movements are more complex, tactical training is difficult to coordinate with physical training, and needs can vary widely among individuals. These coaches have experience working with some of the world's best teams and walk us through their approaches

Throughout both parts of the book some common themes emerge. The more I talk to master coaches, the more I see three themes recur in particular: responsiveness, simplicity, and balance. You see them with sprint coaches. You see them with throws coaches. You see them with soccer coaches. You see them with endurance coaches. No matter how diverse your sample, great coaches stick to these principles, and this book seeks to show how a set of core principles can be actualized in different ways and situations.

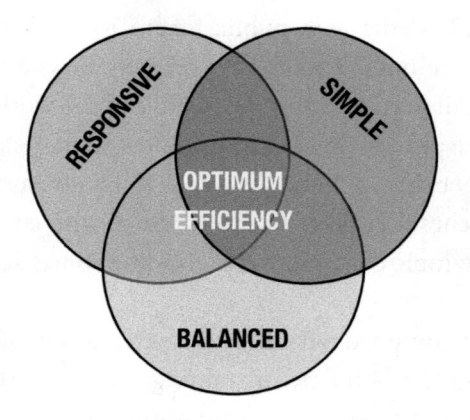

Introduction

RESPONSIVE TRAINING

Testing and monitoring has become an essential part of training, but what differentiates the top coaches is that they understand the need for testing. The point of a test is not the result. As coaches, the only result we care about, in the end, is the result on the field. The point of testing is to see if our training worked.

If I am testing my athlete's jumping ability, or maximum in a weight room exercise, I care less about how high they jump or how much they lift, than whether or not the value has improved. It may look like I am testing the athlete, but I am really testing the plan to see whether it worked. If they improved, then my plan just might have worked. If not, it is time to go back to the drawing board since, no matter how strong they are, my plan failed. As was the case in school, testing is where we learn whether we passed or failed as coaches. The best coaches, then, respond to their result with their future training plans.

Training must be responsive, and a test is one thing that coaches can respond to. But there are many other ways to gather data to make decisive decisions. As Vern Gambetta often says, testing is training and training is testing; simply getting good feedback from training can help you make better decisions without the need for extra testing. Bondarchuk has the simplest approach in this regard: every day he measures how far his athletes throw and uses that to tailor future training. He uses an objective measure of the athlete's form today to optimize training tomorrow.

The testing is training approach is easier to apply in some sports than others, something Derek Evely discusses in our interview. But where there is a will, there's a way. Dave Tenney, Tom Myslinski, and John Pryor all discuss how technology is helping them get a better grasp on the quality and quantity of training in field sports.

All of these approaches focus on objective feedback, but recent research has shown the value and effectiveness of subjective feedback from the ath-

TRAINING TALK

lete. Asking athletes how they feel is far easier than giving them a series of tests, and now we're learning it might be more accurate too. The modern search for data has tried to make our analysis more objective, but more data also means more false data and more time and expertise required to sift through the haystack to find the needle. Both John Kiely and Dan Pfaff list education as one key tenet in their training philosophy for this very reason. If the athlete is educated on what they are doing and why they are doing it, then they will be able to provide better feedback on how to move forward and help the coach find the most valuable data.

No matter whether you are making decisions based on objective or subjective information, it is important that it is information measuring the right thing. For example, gathering endurance data for decision-making with a power athlete will not help them get better at their sport. Therefore coaches like Bondarchuk and Pfaff encourage an analytic approach to define what matters for your sport and your athletes. Pfaff talks about defining key performance indicators; Bondarchuk focuses on classifying the sporting movements. No matter the method, coaches need to define their sport before they define their tests. Only after that can you start looking for where the right data is hiding.

SIMPLE TRAINING

As we have seen with the example of responsiveness, more complex is not always better. Simple data is not just easier to use, it can also be more effective. Measuring a throw or asking an athlete how they feel are very simple approaches, but they are also powerful enough to produce world records. This is not the only area of training where simplicity rules.

Successful coaches seem to use a variation of Occam's razor: if there are two ways to do something, the simplest is the best. John Pryor provides the best example of this when he explained the strategies he used to help Japan rugby reach historic success at the 2015 World Cup. Rugby is a complex sport, but as the problem becomes more complex, Pryor found the solution has to become simpler. His athletes have to sprint in mul-

Introduction

tiple directions with a variety of random obstacles coming at them. To address that he focuses on just one or two key points. Bosch expanded on this concept in his interview, stating that the most specific approach is often the general approach that focuses on simple abilities that can be applied in more situations.

Another simple truth about training is that it is also as much about how the method is delivered than the method itself. As John Kiely details, how much an athlete believes in the plan can determine its effectiveness. And we all know the large role that communication plays in coaching. You can have all the know-how in the world, but it is communication that really counts. You have to be able to communicate it to the athlete in order for it to help. And, as Albert Einstein said, "If you can't explain it simply, you don't understand it well enough." For this reason, much of Harry Marra's interview focuses on the art of coaching and how to improve communication by making it simpler. He had to prepare Ashton Eaton for 10 events; complex communication was not an option. Watch the top coaches at the Olympics and often not a word will pass between them and their athletes. This is simplicity at its finest.

Simplicity does not mean easy. Many times the simple approach can mean more work. A key element of Bondarchuk's philosophy is transfer of training: do the training that will help you improve in your sport. This is the simplest of concepts, but it requires work to define what that training is.

When Derek Evely describes how he breaks down each exercise, we can see how the importance of specificity permeates into every training decision. Dan Pfaff spends a large amount of time defining key performance indicators for his athletes and tailoring training accordingly. Even in field sports, Tom Myslinski and Dave Tenney have been at the forefront of identifying the individual needs of each player and position in American football and soccer with the help of new technology. Defining the needs of each player requires work, but it is rooted in a simple concept: wide receivers and offensive linemen require different types of training.

TRAINING TALK

It is the simple then, not always the easy, that coaches are after. For many coaches, this search brings them back to the start of their coaching career. As we try something new we see the big picture and it all looks so simple. For example, sprinting is simply about getting from point A to B as fast as possible. As we gain competence, we start to understand all the details behind this initial layer: sprinting is about stride length and frequency; it is about science and physics; it is about force production and ground reaction force; it is about a complex interplay of different elements. Eventually, coaches are able to take a step back and see the simplicity again.

In the end, sprinting is just about getting somewhere fast. The master coaches understand that and keep that in mind with everything they do. Read Pat Connolly's training philosophy, and you see it is simple. For each training element, she asks if it is specific or whether it helps prevent injury. If not, she doesn't use it. For the master coaches, the solution is simple. This is how mastery works in any endeavor: taking something simple, unravelling it, and then making it simple again.

BALANCED TRAINING

The final element I see among master coaches is balance. The traditional approach to training is to build physical qualities separately and, only later, put them together. First you build size, then strength, and then speed. The difficulty is that it can be hard to reassemble different parts at the end of the year, when each element was built separately. You get a Frankenstein monster that may look impressive, but lacks basic functionality.

If you look at the training of Vern Gambetta, Dan Pfaff, Frans Bosch, and others in the book, they often try to build up an athlete's skills in parallel. Speed is trained along with strength and size. When elements are built up together it helps ensure they fit together and work properly together. Even Bondarchuk, well known for advocating specific strength and specific exercises in training, includes exercises from all ends of the spectrum in every training session.

Introduction

In fact, when you train things separately you are sometimes training two separate things. As John Pryor detailed, if players are running slower in training, the timing of passes and tactic trained are completely different than what they want to see in the game.

At a smaller scale, the body also learns better when working together. We can break a movement down into parts and train each muscle separately, but it is not always wise to do so. As Vern Gambetta often says, we need to train movements, not muscles. Competition movements always have to be performed in their entirety, and breaking them down into smaller drills often takes away this connectedness. Every coach interviewed highlighted this point.

How you find balance can be counter-intuitive. If you always stand on firm ground, you might think you have balance, but you will tumble at the slightest change of surface. Always doing the same thing can give you a false sense of balance. True balance comes from destabilizing the athlete. As Bosch explains, "It is through variation that technique truly stabilizes." The goal, however, always remains balance: a balanced body, a balanced mind, and a balanced plan.

DOING THE MOST WITH THE LEAST

If you take a step back, you can further consolidate these three points into just one element: efficiency. If your training is not responsive, you will waste time going down the wrong path. Bondarchuk mentions how the biggest advantage to his approach is not necessarily his methods, but the fact that he can get feedback more often, allowing him to find out what works and eliminate inefficiencies.

Simplicity is, by definition, efficient. If training and communication are not simple, you waste time and effort on the wrong methods or on a message that is not getting through to the athlete.

Balance is also about efficiency. By building up the athlete together, you save yourself the work of putting the pieces together. By training move-

TRAINING TALK

ments rather than muscles, the body finds the most efficient way to link its parts and solve the puzzle you present it.

But, efficiency is much broader than just these three points. It is a mindset about doing the most with the least. A quote from Henk Kraiijenhof came up in the interview with Dan Pfaff and encapsulates the goal, "I try to see how little we can do and still be great." That is what efficiency is about.

Efficiency is the name of the game in modern elite sports, and one of the principles that all of these coaches consider part of their core beliefs. But not every topic discussed in this book has such universal acceptance. Obviously, each coach interviewed has his or her own philosophy and own plan; they likely disagree on as many elements as they agree. It is in how the points are applied that the differences emerge. But as a coach you can even learn from these elements. If you stay within your comfort zone and never challenge your beliefs, it will be impossible to progress. It is only by confronting new people and new concepts from a variety of backgrounds that you can test your approach and see if it holds water or not. My first mentor, Harold Connolly, weighing 250 pounds at the time, even took ballet lessons to learn about movement and rhythm from a new perspective. You will reject many more ideas than you accept, but the process of being exposed to and evaluating new ideas is how we learn.

Just before I finished this book, I passed along one of the interviews to a friend of mine. He replied simply with one quote from philosopher Jean-Paul Sartre:

> Acting is a question of absorbing other people's personalities and adding some of your own experience.

Coaching is a question of absorbing other people's training and adding some of your own experience. So, take an inside look at how these coaches train athletes, and see what you can add from your own experience.

PART I //

AT THE TRACK

TRACK AND FIELD is one of the world's oldest sports for a reason: it is sport at its most basic level. Broken down, track and field is simply about who can run the fastest, jump the highest or longest, and throw the farthest. The sport was the highlight of the ancient Olympics, and we can be assured that even cavemen had footraces and competitions to see who could throw rocks farther. Running, jumping, and throwing are the basic elements of movement, and nearly every sport is built upon at least one of these elements.

It is clear, then, why some of the most influential figures in physical preparation have a background in track and field. Most modern training and planning methods were developed and refined in the sport. Some of the first athletes to utilize periodization, for example, were in track and field. Weightlifting, as a supplemental exercise, was also adopted by track and field throwers before many other sports opened their eyes to its benefits.

As a hammer thrower, I am obviously biased to the training theories and practices that have come out of track and field. Surely, we can learn from any sport, as Vern Gambetta pointed out in the foreword, but we can learn a lot in particular from the top track and field coaches. The wealth of accumulated knowledge in the sport has produced some great ideas and great coaches.

One of the reasons track and field has proved to be such a fertile testing ground of training methods is because it is so straightforward. A runner has the goal to simply run faster. A basketball player, on the other hand,

TRAINING TALK

focuses on improving jumping ability, speed, agility, as well as technical elements like shooting, passing, dribbling, and defending. Subsequently, figuring out what training will help a basketball player is more difficult. With so many elements it is also difficult to tell if the training is the reason for playing better. The direct link between training and performance in track and field helps coaches quickly identify what works and what doesn't. Then these principles can be applied to other sports.

In this section of the book, I interview some of the leading track and field coaches with a wide range of experience. I begin with the broadest perspective from Vern Gambetta. After starting as a coach in the decathlon, Gambetta has taken these concepts on to train elite athletes in dozens of sports. Harry Marra used to train alongside Gambetta. While he focuses on just one event, also the decathlon, it is the event that includes nearly every movement in the sport. Both Gambetta and Marra share a great overview of the art of coaching and the best approach to training.

In my interviews with Gary Winckler, Dan Pfaff, and Pat Connolly, we jump into more details on training methods. Winckler is a one of the world's best hurdles coaches, Pfaff has coached world champions in a variety of events from sprinting to field events, and Connolly guided some of the best female sprinters in history. All are respected well beyond their sport.

To finish off this part, we look a bit at knowledge coming out of the world of throwing. My coach, Dr. Anatoliy Bondarchuk, is a leader in sports-specific training methods and periodization. Canadian coach Derek Evely, who has combined his concepts with those of other top coaches, does a great job at helping explain how to successfully put Bondarchuk's theory into practice. Combined, these seven coaches share insight into training methods and philosophies from the world of track and field. It takes little imagination to see how to apply them to a variety of other sports.

Although track and field was a forerunner in terms of physical preparation, what also makes the sport stand out is that it is always moving forward. The constant competition among young athletes drives progress. This is interesting because constant competition in the business world does not always provide the same result. Many of the companies that used to be leaders in innovation become complacent once they achieve success. A quick look at the world of technology will give you hundreds of names of once-successful companies that now no long exist. Examples include Netscape and Compuserve and, more recently, Blackberry and Nokia have become former innovators struggling to survive. Complacency is part of human nature, but it shows itself the most among larger groups. The effort to get a big organization to try something different is harder to summon than the effort to do it alone.

This is where track and field has another advantage. Some of the biggest success stories in the sport have just one athlete and one coach behind them. A small team allows for easy experimentation. When you have that dynamic playing out across the world, new ideas constantly emerge. In this part of the book you will see for yourself how the sport keeps moving itself forward and what these leading coaches developed in their laboratory of ideas.

1 // VERN GAMBETTA

Often described as the coach of coaches, Vern Gambetta has been a leading coach and educator for five decades. Starting out as a decathlete and multi-events coach, he has since progressed to coaching athletes in nearly every track and field event and, for that matter, nearly every sport.

In the 1980s, after cofounding the USATF coaching education program, he left the sport to work in strength and conditioning for a series of professional teams in baseball, basketball, and other sports including the Chicago White Sox, New York Mets, and the US men's national soccer team.

Gambetta continues to consult with various professional clubs and federations, but he is currently more focused on coaching education. He runs the GAIN coaching network and annual workshop, cohosts the popular GAINcast podcast and has written several books including the best-selling *Athletic Development: The Art & Science of Functional Sports Conditioning*.

When I talked to Gambetta in 2011 for this interview, we had only met once before; but his common sense approach to general training principles has kept me returning to him when I want a second opinion of new training methods or ideas. Since then he has become one of the biggest influences on my coaching.

TRAINING TALK

While I use some training methods inspired by him, the biggest influence he has had on my training is in simply shaping my critical approach to coaching and learning. In other words, what I have taken from him is a general training philosophy which he helps explain in this interview through examples from his decades of experiences at the highest levels of sport.

LESSONS TO LEARN

- The whole is stronger than its parts. The body is an amazing thing and gains strength when segments link together to form a kinetic chain. Therefore, in training it is important to keep the kinetic chain in mind. By working individual elements in training you not only break up the rhythm of the sport but risk creating injury by creating imbalance between the links.

- The contemporary reality in sports requires that you train all qualities at all times. If you take too much time away from one need, you will require even more time to recover your former baseline there. Especially in technical sports, you should never be that far away from the competitive movement. The proportions spent on each quality can vary over the season, but all should be ever present.

- General coordination skills are undervalued. Many coaches focus on building strength as a base, but coordination underlies everything. The more pathways you can open, the more connections you can make.

FOCUS ON MOVEMENTS, NOT MUSCLES

MB: **You are well known for advocating training technique and strength in parallel. I agree, and I see this separation not just in training, but also in drills where people will break the throw into parts. The hammer is about rhythm and connecting the turns together. If you do a drill that breaks up this rhythm it is hard to bring back together. My coach, Anatoliy Bondarchuk, has strong opinions on this, but he is an outlier among throws coaches. How is the consensus in other events?**

GAMBETTA: I see this with each event right now. I think it has something to do with what I call "internet training porn." People can put up all these wacko drills on YouTube and try to impress each other. I am working on a presentation now, and I've been putting together five of the dumbest drills I've seen like throwing the shot from your knees. Why? It makes no sense. Throw the shot. Throw a lighter shot. Throw a heavier shot. What are you working on?

TRAINING TALK

I just spent some time with Jerry Clayton, the [former] throws coach at Auburn, after he came back from the World Championships. He said the only people you saw doing drills there were the American throwers. The drills break things into too many parts. Here again Bondarchuk opened my eyes.

A few years ago I was working with a post-collegiate elite heptathlete after her coach recommended she visit me for some training. The first day we are out with the shot put I just watched as she spent 15 minutes doing drills. I stopped her, gave her the shot, and told her to just throw the shot so that I could see what she could do. She had a drill for her wrist, a drill for everything and that's the way her throw ended up looking. After that, we just worked on full throws to put it together.

That, right now, is killing us. It's killing us in the sprints, the jumps, every event. Similar is not the same. That's what we have to remember. Just because it looks like the event, the dynamics are different, and we have to be acutely aware of that. As you can tell, I get pretty fired up about this because I've made those mistakes. It's one of the lessons I learned when Tom Tellez invited me to come down and spend three days with him during my last year at Cal Berkeley. I watched Carl Lewis train and didn't see three drills in three days; and then you cross-reference to Bondarchuk and others.

>> *Similar is not the same . . . Just because it looks like the event, the dynamics are different, and we have to be acutely aware of that.*

If the drills are done for a specific purpose and they are not form drills, but rather special strength drills, then it is another story. It is not that you don't do drills, but your range is very narrow and you have to make sure it doesn't cause neural interference with your event.

MB: **One of the principles you list as a "systemic sport development principle" is to train movements, not muscles. Is this related?**

GAMBETTA: Sure. That point was first meant in terms of strength training. If you go back and look at the early strength training methodology used in track and field, there was a big bodybuilding influence. The brain doesn't recognize individual muscles; it doesn't break things into parts. It looks for muscle synergies, flow, rhythm, and tempo. If you look at all the throws, not just the hammer throw, there is a certain rhythm and tempo governed by the weight of the implement, size of the athlete, size of the circle, etc. You cannot have an undue focus just on parts.

> \>\> *The brain doesn't recognize individual muscles; it doesn't break things into parts. It looks for muscle synergies, flow, rhythm and tempo.*

MB: **When you started working with baseball and basketball and other sports, you were one of the first people in that type of position and got to develop a lot from scratch. Did you find it easier to implement the "movements not muscles" mentality since they didn't have methods that grew out of bodybuilding?**

GAMBETTA: To a certain extent, but when you look at baseball, they tend to look at just the arm and shoulder. Luckily, parallel to the time I started to get involved, the biomechanist Dr. Chuck Dillman started biomechanical analysis of pitchers and explained the concept of the kinetic chain to our coaches. They bought in, but that was just within the White Sox organization.

When you are sailing uncharted waters, people sometimes look at you like you have two heads, but when you start to have success they notice. The first thing we noticed is that the injuries just stopped. I've seen the same

TRAINING TALK

applying this to swimming. Look at the kinetic chain and see how effectively you are connecting the links. Then ask if you need to strengthen, lengthen, or make other changes to make the body more connected.

MB: **What are the elements of training this aspect?**

GAMBETTA: It's the things I've read on your blog. It's what Bondarchuk and Klaus Bartonietz talk about. I think it's also throwing left-handed, as you saw some of in the famous Werner Günthör training video. That is something we even did with our pitchers the day after they threw for the cross-education effect.

I think there is still a lot of room in all of the throws for exploring general coordination. Tumbling, trampoline, and other types of general gymnastics moves can be used to improve body awareness and relationships. I do think the multi-throws, throwing various weighted implements, right- and left-handed throws, etc. all help enhance connection.

The current thinking about skill acquisition and motor learning would say that you shouldn't do that; but my experience tells me that the more pathways I can open, the more connections I can make. Then, when I get to my specific activity, the better I will be at it. That's how I would approach it.

MB: **You also write a lot about posture. Can you talk a little about that in general, the role of posture in training?**

>> *Posture is how things connect.*

GAMBETTA: Again, posture is how things connect. We tend to think of posture as a still picture. When you look at a movement, it is a series of postures. To me this is the unifying element that goes hand in glove with the concept of training movements and not muscles.

What is your posture at release? There is a real strong core component to it, but there is also a component of how things connect and how things work together. Posture and rhythm are two unifying elements that connect everything. Posture is where your head is and how your center is aligned in regard to your base of support will determine your success or failure. Your posture in the hammer throw as you initiate your first turn is crucial. If you are hinged or bent at the waist, it just isn't going to happen. It is absolutely crucial and must be trained and threaded throughout your strength training and all your elements of training.

OFFSEASON & PRESEASON TRAINING

MB: **I was talking with Jean-Pierre Egger, the coach of world champion shot putters Werner Günthör and Valerie Adams, a few months ago and asked him what he would have done differently with Günthör. Egger has had a similar career path as you have, working with various sports after Günthör retired. With all his experience, he said the he wouldn't have changed much about the technique, but he would have spent less time building a base when training started up each year in the fall. I've heard that from quite a few athletes now.**

GAMBETTA: We are operating in the wrong paradigm. When I look at an athlete's program and it says "preparation period" or "general preparation," I see an antiquated model, and the coaching programs still teach this. You should never get very far away from the competitive implement. I heard a young American throws coach at a convention a few years ago, and he said, "We don't touch an implement for the first six to eight weeks of training; we just lift really heavy to build a better strength base." And I'm thinking then it will take you another six to eight weeks to get back to your technical model. You need to train all elements all the time in different proportions. That is contemporary thought and what the best coaches do in all sports.

Dedicated periods of general preparation don't work; you thread them into the rest of training. It is interesting to hear Egger said that because it

TRAINING TALK

is the same conclusion I came to. Every year with my athletes, we would go back in the fall to these periods, and I call it dulling the knife. They started razor sharp, and we just dulled it for three months. We took away the fine coordination they had.

> **>> *You should never get very far away from the competitive implement.***

MB: **Do you use any type of general preparation period now, or do you jump into combining everything at once?**

GAMBETTA: Just like injury prevention and other elements of training, it should be threaded throughout training. I was talking to Jerry Clayton about this the other day and we talked about, "resetting the system." If you finish something with a real technical emphasis, you can go two or three days working on balance stuff to work on calming the nervous system down and taking the load off. Instead of putting blocks of time in, you put elements of it in.

MB: **Did you notice a difference when you started switching to that method with your athletes?**

GAMBETTA: Yes; I didn't have to hesitate. There was a smoother transition. We used to talk about the X model: moving from high volume and low intensity to low volume and high intensity. We always said the biggest danger zone was at the X where they crossed. But we didn't have the little niggling injuries when we used volume and intensity in parallel at high levels.

There is a famous swim coach named Gennadi Touretski who used to coach Alexander Popov. I remember him saying on my first trip to Australia that his swimmers should be able to dive in the pool anytime, any day, and be within a certain percentage of their personal best. When I was an athlete, we would do all this slow volume training in the fall and then do a pentathlon to test our form with a long jump, 200 meters, and some other events. It felt like running in wet concrete. I thought, "This is really stupid and we should rethink this." This was in 1972. It took me a while to really figure it out.

MB: **How long was the rest period for most of your athletes when you were coaching them hands on?**

GAMBETTA: Too long! I wouldn't do that now. I'd say "I'll see you in a month," but you can't afford to do that now and compete at a high level. When I coached high school I had some really good distance and middle distance runners. I tried to make them take a month off, but I caught them running all the time. They were smarter than their coach. They were thinking, "Why should I take a month off? I just ran in the state meet and feel sharp. I should be reinforcing that." That doesn't mean that you need to compete. You can let the nerves rest and muscles work. If you look around, you don't see people doing this much anymore, taking the long forced rest breaks.

FUTURE ADVANCES IN TRAINING & TECHNOLOGY

MB: **You can't talk about training nowadays without talking about technology. There are several ways it is impacting training. First, you have technology giving people better access to knowledge. The average high school coach can learn more easily nowadays with the availability of information online. Then you have technology helping with injuries and rehabilitation through new medical treatments. And you also have technology providing more detailed feedback and data. The cameras are better; runners can use high tech watches to provide all sorts of details about training runs that you just couldn't do before.**

With training methods, names like Anatoliy Bondarchuk, Tom Tellez, Arthur Lydiard are still dominant even though their biggest advancements were a long time ago. Do you see any big advancements in training methods that I have missed or that are on the horizon?

TRAINING TALK

GAMBETTA: I've really been looking into new technologies, but as far as training systems or training methods, I'm just seeing the new technologies simply going in and verifying why some of these methods that have worked actually do work.

I think we'll see the big breakthroughs in technique by looking at how we help athletes process the information in making technical changes with more feedback. Another big area will be monitoring training: monitoring the effects of a strength training workout neurally and metabolically.

There are some really new innovations, but most of them are in relation to monitoring training. The cryosauna needs research, but there are some coaches and scientists I really respect that have anecdotally said that it works, especially for collision sports. Will it help a hammer thrower speed up their recovery? I don't know, but for a player right now at the Rugby World Cup, I'd give it a try as long as I don't get frostbite.

One idea that should make us take a note is the central governor theory put out by South African Tim Noakes. That will make us take a look at how we are training our distance and middle-distance people.

In terms of the other events, this monkey see, monkey do syndrome worries me. I can do a Google search right now and come up with 50 different videos on the long jump. This is an advantage compared to when it used to take weeks to obtain information, but is also a downside. Somebody can just come up with an off-the-wall idea and there is no filter.

We live in exciting times, and I do think there will be some innovations, but I don't know what they are now. What do you feel as an athlete? Do you see anything on the horizon?

MB: **What I see a lot of, since I am involved with it on my site, is the proliferation of information. Before Bondarchuk moved to North America, e.g., only a handful of his articles with little substance had been translat-**

ed into English, and most of what people knew about him was based on (mostly wrong) hearsay. Now, I see that people are reading his books, attending seminars, etc. More people are learning "new" ideas from him and others, but they are not necessarily new ideas.

GAMBETTA: What is his opinion about it? Does he see anything big on the horizon?

MB: When I say Bondarchuk is among the old ideas group, that isn't necessarily correct. He is still collecting data from his current throwers, reanalyzing his older data, writing articles and books, and adjusting how his training plans are put together.

Bondarchuk's training is not a static concept. What he did in 1972 with himself is different than what he did in 1980 with Sedykh, different than 1986 with Sedykh, different than the 1990s, and also different than his current training group.

GAMBETTA: That's part of the reason I have so much respect for him and Gary Winckler. Gary hasn't ever gone 180° about face; great coaches never do that, but he is constantly reevaluating his approach. There is a guy I didn't mention, Frans Bosch, who has looked at sprinting and running with different eyes. That is where the innovation is also coming. By looking at the same thing with different and new eyes, we will get new ideas. But, there is no one doing research on the throws in this country, virtually none, and very little in athletics as a whole.

MB: Throughout your career, you've worked with essentially every major sport and every track and field event. Having seen such a broad landscape of training and coaching, what are some things we can learn from each other?

GAMBETTA: The way to get maximal power in training is to release the implement, and what throwers do well is incorporating releases of vari-

TRAINING TALK

ous forms into training. Some people have taken to calling this the multi-throw, but it is just ballistic training. If you take a heavy implement like the bench press, you are only accelerating that weight for a short period of time, and then you have to decelerate it to stop it even if you are moving it fast. If you don't release the implement, you won't achieve maximum power production.

What I saw when I was training for decathlon in Santa Barbara, and a lot of the Europeans would come over to train, was that they didn't spend anywhere near the time we spent in the weight room. Now these were decathletes, but they could throw because they had the ballistic ability to really accelerate the implement. They would throw heavy implements like 20 kg weight plates. That is one of the things that, particularly European throwers, do very well going back several decades. And the hammer throwers showed us the way on that more than anyone else.

Regardless of the sport, you have to come back to the demands of the event. The unifying element of each of the throws is that you are trying to find optimum release velocity. When you look at a spectrum of strength and power training, you will emphasize different elements at different times, but it will always come back to speed. A mistake we make with young throwers is to add strength first. Now, especially American throwers, get too focused on chasing numbers in the weight room. Let's get really good coordination and refine their model by developing their strength and technique in parallel. For me, working on coordinative capacities is the key and there are a lot of throwers in the world who have done this: Andreas Thorkildsen, Jan Zelezny, and Werner Günthör.

2 // HARRY MARRA

Despite serving as the US national decathlon team coach for a decade and coaching six men over 8,000 points, Harry Marra was a relative unknown outside of the insulated world of multi-events when he joined the University of Oregon before the 2010 season. He was hired with one purpose: to guide a talented, 21-year-old decathlete named Ashton Eaton. Ashton had already qualified for the national team at the 2009 World Championships, but he needed continued development in several events in order to compete with the world's best.

Over the next three seasons, Eaton set the NCAA record, won the Bowerman award, improved the world indoor heptathlon record three times, broke the world decathlon record, and claimed Olympic golds in London and Rio. His wife, Canadian Brianne Theisen Eaton, also flourished under Marra. Theisen Eaton broke the Canadian record, won the Commonwealth Games and World Indoor Championships, as well as silver at the World Championships and bronze in Rio. After Marra was named as the USATF national coach of the year in 2012, and won the IAAF Coaching Achievement Award in 2016, few people will overlook him again.

While some coaches are well known for their training methods or their technical model, Marra is a master of the soft skills. Specifically, he is a master communicator. The decathlon is a complex sport where athletes

TRAINING TALK

must master 10 varied tasks and recite them flawlessly over little more than 24 hours. The only way to be successful in such a sport is to simplify everything.

In 2013, I was able to get Marra to visit Zurich to put on a clinic. Beforehand we sat down for this interview on the theme of that clinic: the art of coaching. He explains the necessity of simple communication and how to develop cues that work best for each athlete. The art of coaching is also woven into the program, so he provided some examples of how he develops a weekly plan for a complex sport requiring athletes to master 10 distinct skills.

LESSONS TO LEARN

- Simple cues work better, but simple cues are not easy to create. You start out making sure you are on the same page as the athlete, and then, simplify as much as possible until you get to the core point you are working on in the most compact and easiest-to-understand form.

- Communication is a two-way street. Communication is not just about talking; the athlete needs to understand and implement what you are saying. Therefore, as a coach, you need to listen to them to see what they like, what they understand, and what they feel. This is the best feedback in creating good cues.

- Efficiency is the key to injury prevention in sports where you must train many different physical qualities. Find exercises that work two or more things at once. For example, medicine ball throws help develop throwing technique while also promoting overall coordination and explosiveness that will help in the jumps and sprints.

THE ART OF COACHING

MB: **When you talk about the art of coaching, a key point you focus on is simplicity: you have to use simple and effective cues with an athlete. For Ashton in London, you had just 18 words that covered all 10 events. What process do you have in creating a cue for one of your athletes?**

MARRA: Well if you look at it backwards, in the end the cue becomes a word or two or three. It will be just a short little phrase or statement to the athlete. Something like, "Keep your legs underneath you." Where it starts is when the training starts for the year each fall. The discussion between the coach and the athlete is very broad at that point.

Let's say we are working on the shot put. First we are trying to make sure each of us is on the same page regarding terminology and concepts in the shot put. Once that is aligned through communication back and forth—it is important that it is not just coming from the coach—the communication becomes more solid and the verbiage used to describe something becomes a much more compact statement. That's the big picture: it is very,

TRAINING TALK

very broad in the fall, and then it becomes more narrow and focused as you move into the competition season.

MB: **Finding a cue is the most important step, but one thing I find when coaching is that after awhile the cues go stale, and you need a new cue in order to keep progressing on the same technical point. Do you experience that and, if so, how do you address that?**

MARRA: You always have to keep the line of communication going between the athlete and coach in all aspects, especially in the decathlon since there are so many damn problems that can come up. The cues can change even as you are in your final preparation for a major meet, when you realize that a different cue might work better.

> \>\> *What you have to realize is that the final cue should really come from the athlete.*

What you have to realize is that the final cue should really come from the athlete. I'll ask "What are you feeling on that throw?" If he answers that he feels he is loading his big right toe, then I'll use it since I know that's what gets him to respond and post up better during the throw. You jot that down in your notebook and, then, try to understand what he means by that. You might also have a second way of analyzing it if the first throw doesn't go well and he is a bit lost. But the cue should come from the athlete, and, you're right, the cues should change. Perhaps in your event, or with a single event athlete, it might not change as often. A multi-event athlete might practice the javelin one or two times a week. When you come back to it, you have to think about where you left off.

MB: **I see that with some of my younger athletes, I get them for hammer throw technical work just once a week, and much of the practice is then** spent getting back to where we were at the end of the last practice. Only at the end do we finally take a few steps forward. With them, I can use the same cue for a year. But with the more advanced athletes, we get so specific in the technique that we often need to try working at problems from a new approach.

MARRA: You are right. One thing that is critical, and I'm just thinking out loud here, is that, in designing the cue, the coach needs to know all the demands that are on the athlete for the event. You have to know all of them so that you can design, or help the athlete design, a cue that will be helpful for him or her. But no matter what, every coach also needs a fundamental understanding of their event.

MB: **As an example of this, you've described how you refined Ashton's long jump cues throughout the past year and ended up with a single word at the end of last season: "perpendicular." Can you walk us through what the broad focus was at the start of the season and how it came to end with that final simple one-word cue?**

MARRA: The concept in the long jump and the 100 meters last season was consistency. He pretty much understood how to do both events, but we needed to find the consistency. This is especially important in the decathlon, since you only get three attempts in the long jump. A normal jumper might get off one decent jump and two fouls in a meet, but that is good enough for him to make finals and get three more chances to clean up technique and timing. In the multi-events, you don't have that margin of error.

Obviously, an important part of the long jump and how you start out of the back relies on the running posture and making sure you have a full foot under you, instead of being just on the toes. You also need to make sure you are driving off your left and onto the penultimate and then off of the board. As a coach, I watch that. But, if the athlete is doing that all well like Ashton, I throw it out and don't even go back to that or remind the athlete of that since it is working. Instead I just remind him of one thing:

TRAINING TALK

stay perpendicular. This reminds him to keep it perpendicular over the last three steps. In other words, keep your upper body sitting right over the lower body. Don't lean forward. Don't lean back. If you do that after you have done all the other stuff on the approach, 99% of the time you will not foul, and you will be in a great position to apply force to the board.

MB: **When you were starting out the season, was the cue much longer than that?**

MARRA: Absolutely; it was a concept thing. It was understanding that maybe the back part of the runway was good, but he was too cautious in the middle. We worked on all of those phases and then focused on the rhythm of the last three steps. Once that got better, all of a sudden he was running to the board rather than through the board. We know that's not good; you have to run through the board. Now all the phases are pretty good; we left them alone and then focused on keeping perpendicular. This gave him a lot of confidence that his foot would be right underneath him and he wouldn't foul. I don't know if you have ever long jumped, but if you are cautious of fouling, you will take a lot of speed off the release.

MB: **I haven't long jumped, but I can imagine that if you hesitate a little the rhythm is just gone. It's the same in all events.**

>> *In every event, I think it is always better to be slow and in the correct positions to apply forces than fast and out of position.*

MARRA: Yeah. In every event I think it is always better to be slow and in correct positions to apply forces than fast and out of position. If you are out of position, you cannot apply forces to build on it. In the long jump, if you are a little off the board and in good position, you are better off than reaching to get on the board and being in a bad position to jump. Ashton took off a good foot before the board in Estonia in 2011 and still jumped 7.77 meters. That's when we knew his long jump could be good, once we ironed out the takeoff.

MB: **You have said you just have 18 cues for Ashton for all 10 of his events. Are those just the cues you use in competition, or do you have additional cues you are also using in training?**

MARRA: Sometimes in a training cycle, if the shot put or high jump is going bad, we will have a discussion and try to come up with a better understanding of it and maybe, the cues change. But we use those, then, for both competition and practice.

Ashton told me straight up when I arrived that he did not want more than three cues per event. That was good communication right there, since he let me know he couldn't handle more than that. In discus his cue is, "Firm on the left out of the back." We just keep it that simple. An ideology I have is that if you start a skill correctly, for instance start the long jump approach correctly or start off the discus balanced, then you put yourself in a position to be successful. If you start improperly you will pick up speed across the ring, but all you can hope for is that you are a good enough athlete to just overcome those mistakes.

MB: **That leads into the next question. Ashton has just one or two cues per event, but that is 18 total cues to think about over a two-day competition. I can't imagine trying to have 18 things to focus on, even if it was just one or two per event. Does that ever get to be too much?**

MARRA: No. Your question begs to what the decathlon is all about. It's about focus and concentration. Here's what we do: the morning of the first day we just focus on the first event, the 100 meters. The focus is entirely on that and you are focusing on your 100-meter cues. After the 100 meters, you take a break, rest, and put your feet up. Before you start your warm up

TRAINING TALK

for the next event, the long jump, we take out our cues and he goes over them. Then he is a long jumper, nothing else at that point. That is how we work it throughout all the events.

TRAINING FOR A COMPLEX SPORT

MB: **My next questions are about training for a complex event like a decathlon. Training is relatively simple in the hammer throw; I can address all points of training at each training session. But when you are training for 10 events, that isn't the case. You were saying that you might work once or twice a week on some of the throwing events. Is that typical for all the events? How does that affect the technical development?**

MARRA: The whole thing is set up on one word: safety. The decathlon is an injury looking for a place to happen. You cannot be cranking out long jumps on Monday morning and then coming back to sprinting in the afternoon. You are asking the legs to do too much. You have to find a way to get all the events in and blend them while keeping safe.

Here is an overview of a typical training week. We work two weeks of hard work like this, and then, the third week is a recovery week. This is the same volume of work technically and event wise, but no running. The running is in the pool, or recovery striding on the grass, but not hard intervals.

Monday: We start in the morning with a solid and thorough warm-up that lasts about 40 minutes, and then, we focus on the shot put for 15-30 minutes. Then, we do a specific warm up for the hurdles and a hurdle session. After a few hours break, we come back in the afternoon and do an easy warm up, high jump practice, and then 400-meter training. That can be a variety of things depending on time of year, but a sample would be 10 x 100 meters with one minute recovery.

Tuesday: We use this as a recovery day for running. Again, we have a thorough warm-up in the morning to flush out any of the excesses from the interval running the previous day. That is a safety valve right there. Then, we focus on the throws. Typically we will do javelin and discus. We do not throw the shot, but before we throw the javelin and discus we will do what I call "shadows" for the shot put. If we had a sticking point technically on Monday, we will work on these, and I will coach him, maybe using some video too and a mirror at the back of the circle. For 15 minutes, we will work on a cue with or without the shot put, but never with a release. We are getting neurological work done even though we are not throwing real hard, since it is a safety thing again. Then, we move on to the discus and javelin and finally strength training.

Wednesday: Again we start with a solid warm up, and then, long jump approaches, takeoffs, and short approaches. After lunch, we do a secondary warm up and train for the pole vault. We finish it off with another intense 400-meter training. Wednesday is one tough day since you have long jumped, pole vaulted, and now you have to run something like four x 300 meters with a short recovery.

Thursday: Another recovery day. We warm-up, as needed, depending on how sore the athlete is. Then we come back to the throws. Except for the shot put on Monday, nearly every throwing practice is done with tired legs. As you know, that is a tough way to learn, but when you come to the ninth event in the decathlon, the javelin, I don't care what type of shape you are in, your legs are not talking to you anymore. You have to learn to throw on tired legs.

The key event to the decathlon, Martin, is the discus. It is not the pole vault or the hurdles or the 400 meters. The reason why is because you have run five events the first day. The second day starts with the hurdles early in the morning, and now, your legs are wobbly as hell, and you get into the discus circle. The first thing that happens is you want to fall into the middle of the circle rather than coming across the circle, and all hell breaks loose.

So, early in the week we try to do the throwing events where there is some life in the legs so we can learn how to do them correctly. Then on Thurs-

TRAINING TALK

day, we try to either shadow them or work on them when they are tired to get that experience. We also do another lifting session.

Friday and Saturday: These are catch-as-catch-can days. Let's say the high jump or pole vault has been a problem, then we come back and fit those events in again, if it is safe. We also lift on Saturday and also do hard hills in the fall and winter on Saturday.

Sunday: Rest day.

MB: **As I mentioned earlier, I find it difficult for athletes to make progress if they are doing an event just once a week, so it is interesting to see how you address that problem. You might train the event just once a week, but you find ways to be creative and develop the skills while doing other activities. That's quite efficient.**

MARRA: Part of the shadows is also our medicine ball program. We use medicine balls almost every day for a variety of reasons. Some people use it for dynamics and explosiveness and multi-throws. We do that, but we also use it every day just to loosen up the whole body and get the tendons strong through repetitions. And it is also another shadow. If I am down with the medicine ball at my hip like a batter, and then, turning and popping the medicine ball against the wall, that is the same action as the throw.

Both Ashton and Brianne were not very good at the medicine ball technique when I first came, and now, they are extremely good at it. Now I say we are cheating work at the shot put, discus, and javelin since we are mimicking them with the medicine ball in our warm-up, and we have to warm up anyway. Now, when they are in the circle, they have a better understanding.

MB: **Are you actively coaching during the medicine ball exercises, or do they just do them?**

MARRA: I am, but not nearly as much as when they first started. It actually just blew me away when I first got to the University of Oregon. It is a top program, but when I said let's do some medicine ball, they didn't have a clue what it was, and when they started throwing it, you could see they were hurting and had no technique and weren't gaining much from it. We had a lot of coaching then, but they have picked it up fast. And once you can do that with a medicine ball, you can bring it over to the circle, and the throws will take off.

MB: **Like you, I think it is important to use exercises that develop both technique and strength at the same time, since you have to have both of them at once in the ring. That leads right into my next question.**

You've talked about both the specificity of training and transference, which are two points that are central to my own training. In the hammer throw the concepts are easier to implement since I can set up my weight room exercises to model the hammer throw. But when you have ten events, it must be harder to develop a strength program that will give you the specific strength needed for all 10 events. Is this done through incorporating medicine balls, or another way? And when you get in the weight room is the work there oriented more towards general or specific strength?

MARRA: I would say compared to throwers, the weight room work is more general. We build the program for any athlete who has finished college with the aim to get stronger in the weight room without adding any weight. This is a safety issue. By adding bulk, you are just carrying it around and asking the body to accept more trauma when you are jumping and hurdling. Our lifting leans towards explosive and dynamic movements. Once conditioning has been established at the start of the year, we finish each exercise from cleans to step-ups with a dynamic movement like pushing a medicine ball against the wall. Everything we are doing is trying to bring the gained strength into something specific.

TRAINING TALK

In the fall we are lifting four days a week with heavier repetitions to strengthen the attachment areas. Two sessions are upper body, and two are lower body. We move to three days a week in January and then twice a week in the late spring focusing more on dynamic exercises and multi-throws. Neither Ashton or Brianne touch the weights at all three weeks prior to the Games. We do just multi-throws, hops, standing long jumps, etc. I, personally, think you need three weeks away from leg work to gain the real dynamic that you need.

MB: **Are you using medicine balls throughout the season then, or just as the season approaches?**

MARRA: We always use them. I have one under my arm wherever we are going. We do things like a double leg hop and push, when holding the medicine ball at the chest. Just the concept of holding the upper body correctly and not letting the ball move you forward and exploding is analogous to other events. Neither of them did that skill very well when they started with me and now they are doing it well and their throws are going better.

On a side note, Ashton is still a little frustrated with the discus. I know he wants 50 meters and I know he can throw 50 meters. He is still a young thrower so when he throws a good one in practice then he goes, "I can really hit this next one," instead of trying to relax a little more.

MB: **Even older throwers have that problem.**

MARRA: When he threw his javelin personal best in March, his first throw was about 60 meters. His second was about 62.60 meters, which was a small personal best. On his third throw, he just tried to relax and it jumped out of his hand and hit 66 meters. The fact that he wasn't trying to throw hard, but instead just tried to hit the right positions, was a bigger eye opener for me than the result.

3 // DAN PFAFF

During the first half of the 20th century it was quite common to see a distance coach working with throwers, or vice versa. Without a big staff of assistant coaches, collegiate track coaches were required to have a much broader skill set. Just look at the biography of the legendary Bill Bowerman as an example. The legendary Oregon coach and Nike co-founder coached Olympians in nearly every event. In my hometown of Seattle, Hec Edmundson not only coached several Olympic medalists on the University of Washington track team, but also guided the basketball team for nearly 30 years. As training has become more specialized, this legacy has been replaced with one-event specialists like myself. But not all coaches are like this and Dan Pfaff is proof that this rare breed still exists.

Pfaff has had unprecedented success across nearly every event including the sprints (1996 Olympic 100-meter gold medalist and former world record-holder Donovan Bailey), jumps (2012 Olympic long jump champion Greg Rutherford), pole vault (2007 World Champion and US record holder Brad Walker), and throws (US discus record holder Suzy Powell). In total he has tutored 49 Olympians.

Pfaff's career has taken him from major universities like Louisiana State University, Texas and Florida to leading the USOC Olympic Training Center in Chula Vista and the UK Athletics High Performance Centre in

TRAINING TALK

London. After the London Olympics, he worked as head coach at Altis, where he grew a world-class coaching staff training group and an innovative coaches education program from scratch.

I have had several chances to sit down with Pfaff, and the following interview is from two separate discussions in 2013 and 2015 where we considered topics including improving technique, his training philosophy, and how common themes appear across multiple events. We also dig deeper and discuss training intensity, density, and in-season programming.

LESSONS TO LEARN

- Training should be enjoyable, educational, and mechanical efficiency should drive the bus. An athlete's key performance indicators must be identified to make sure the focus is correctly set on what they need.

- Generally, programming is too dense with too many training items. A good program should be able to shrink or expand and still work. The goal of a coach is to see how little your athletes can do and still be great. This is true efficiency.

- Knowledge is power. Athletes and coaches improve through knowledge of what they are doing. As a coach, adopting a top-down approach is bound to fail. You do not want silent and ignorant athletes that just follow orders. Knowledgeable athletes become partners and improve the training process.

- In order to work over the long term, training also has to be fun. Athletes will burn out if they do not enjoy their sport. More importantly, coaches will rarely enjoy training if the athletes do not.

IMPROVING TECHNIQUE

MB: I'd like to start off with a question of personal interest to me. I'm curious about your approach to fixing the technical problems of someone with very ingrained bad habits. In other words, how do you teach an old dog, like myself, new tricks?

PFAFF: I think there are two directions from which you can attack problems. If you are looking at film, you can look at frames that occur before the problem and frames that occur after. Sometimes, working on things further down the road can go back and fix the cause. And sometimes, the art is looking at how many frames earlier you have to intervene to get an effectual change at a certain point in time.

A lot of times, the resistance to change is an alarm theory. We set alarms like single support, double support, ball position, time in the air, and so on and so forth. We set up this alarm system for executing movements. These alarms are pretty dominant for elite athletes and override spatial and temporal awareness. Once you are set in a certain pattern, the alarms are the central governor, so to speak.

MB: **How do you approach trying to override these alarms? Will you break down the technique into its component parts?**

TRAINING TALK

PFAFF: I am pretty much a whole movement guy. Drills and part-whole learning have their place as you evolve as an athlete from a beginner to an elite athlete, but I haven't had much success with drills or isolated part-whole integration with advanced athletes. We use real-time tasks.

MB: **So it sounds like you simply want to make things feel different for the body so that it can relearn things without the alarms interfering. What inputs do you use to change the alarms?**

PFAFF: We may change positioning in the circle, the weight of implement, or other entities. If some of the alarms are stuck on the entry of a throw, you can play with shoulder axis, hip axis, deflection angles, where is the head during the wind, etc. There are certain triggers that start the alarm process. Part of the art is figuring out which ones set or reset the alarms.

COMMON THEMES IN COACHING MULTIPLE EVENTS

MB: You've had unprecedented success in a wide range of events, from Donovan Bailey in the 100 meters to Suzy Powell in the discus. What would you say are the core principles in your training across all events?

PFAFF: We don't do things just to do things. Our training is very purposeful and mindful. Everything we do, every component from recovery to work intervals, is done with purpose and for a reason. Too many people slog through training and tick boxes, just to say they do things.

I look at activities as generations on a family tree. Throwing the hammer is first generation for you. Various special strength exercises might be second generation. Prehab or rehabilitation exercises might be third generation. People are doing too much second and third generation. We do real time tasks that add value and are as close to the first generation as possible. And we do them as often as possible throughout the year.

The other problem I see is that a lot of coaches are doing massive general preparation periods or special preparation periods with advanced athletes. It is not my experience, with field events and power-speed sports, that athletes with such a high training age need training phases like that.

MB: **You've been working with world-class athletes for decades. What do you think are some of the things that have changed the most about your approach to training over that time?**

PFAFF: As I've aged, I have gotten more like Henk Kraaijenhof: I try to see how little we can do and still be great. Simplify, and really identify key performance indicators (KPIs) and juggle first generation KPIs as well as you can.

MB: **We'll talk more about KPIs later, but for now I am curious as to how you balance training with someone, like a sprinter, where a high volume of first generation work might be difficult to reach? Are you working up the tree until you find the right mix?**

PFAFF: Another fault we have in sprinting is that we do not ergonomically analyze what is going on. There are different types of work: block starts to overcome inertia, acceleration work, transition into upright sprinting work, upright speed work, and special speed-endurance. Those traits are skills, and if you are going to be good at a skill, you have to do it year round. NBA basketball players are doing starts, stops, sprints, jumps, extended speed, for 10 or 11 months a year, and they do not have higher rate of injury than sprinters using conventional training theory.

I think that the problem lies in dosage and density: how many times a week do you do something and what are the numbers? People are wrapped up in getting nice curves and graphs, but some qualities do not cycle very well, like absolute speed runs. My experience is that kids can only do six of those any time in the year. If you do less, you are not maximizing the training load. If you do more, the speed will drop and you are no longer training the maximum speed. There are some entities that do not cycle, and coaches are trapped in the thought that everything has to undulate or fit in a pie graph. Many of the things we do don't have a lot of variance. Where the variance comes in is the density: how many times in a cycle you do it.

MB: **Derek Evely told me that the biggest thing he learned from you was related to injury prevention and using proper training so that you do not even have to get to the stage where rehabilitation is needed. This is applied differently across different events. Can you explain a little about your general approach here and how it is applied to a specific event or athlete?**

PFAFF: Really early in the game I figured out that injuries stop everything: confidence, trust, evolution, everything. For 42 years of studying, injuries, trends, and patterns have been a huge part of what I do. If you are looking for commonalities, injuries in each event are set up by programming, bad mechanics, and bad sports medicine inputs. These are the three main culprits. I don't think you can be a reductionist and say one takes precedence over another. It is a conspiracy of those three situations that over time create chronicity of injury or bad patterns that lead to injury. These three areas need continued research. Once we find solutions and trends, we need to share so that people can be working together to find solutions.

I do some very basic programming for training, but I use quite big ranges that can be scripted from day-to-day or week-to-week. Too many people get dogmatic about programming. I look at mechanics and trying to be as efficient, simple, and elementary as possible. I try to get brain maps that go in the flow state.

Sports medicine is also the elephant in the room that no one wants to talk about. There are a lot of people going in various directions where sports medicine is not integrated, and not everyone is working from the same page. You have physical therapists doing exercise remediation. Soft tissue people are doing their thing. Osteopaths and chiropractors and acupuncture and anti-aging specialists all get involved. There is so much diversity out there that it is hard for the coach and athlete to be discriminating consumers of sports medicine.

INTENSITY & DENSITY

MB: Something I've noticed, and Derek Evely also pointed out in our training talk, is that quite a few elite athletes seem to be doing a high concentration of maximal intensity work and a high concentration of very low intensity work. Work in the middle is often left out. This is a broad question, but what are your thoughts on that observation?

PFAFF: I think it is a trend, and I think what we are touching on is sympathetic versus parasympathetic responses, pathways, and stimulations. For me, a lot of circuits are done for multiple reasons, whether they are with medicine balls, hurdle mobility circuits, general strength circuits, or specific strength circuits. At first these are loads; when they first learn the circuit, it is a sympathetic response since it is hard and new and novel. There is a lot of focus on trying to learn the task. But after a while it flips biochemically to become parasympathetic in response. I don't think we have the technology yet to define and measure this. But if I had a hunch, in 10 years, we will see how this breaks down into creating sympathetic and parasympathetic responses.

MB: A pole vaulter I was talking to started working with you long-distance. You gave him some medicine ball circuits, and he would blast each exercise. He told me that when you finally met up in person, for the first time, he was surprised that you told him to just ease off and take it easy. What is your approach to the medicine ball circuits you use?

PFAFF: Everyone thinks of medicine balls as a modern phenomenon, but they have been around for hundreds of years. I've seen videos of Swedish students doing medicine ball exercises back in the 1920s similar to what the internet gurus are calling the latest and greatest.

You can use medicine balls for a variety of reasons. You can use them for power training, but we use shot puts and puds for that since we want to throw things far, fast, and explosive. The medicine ball circuits we do for other reasons: fascial movements, parasympathetic recovery, range of

TRAINING TALK

movement, mindfulness, stress reflexology, postural deviations, and other anatomy training purposes.

As guys are going through these movements, there is flexion and extension of the spine, rotation of the spine, and joint sequencing. We look at these factors as a movement screen. We compare turning to the left and right on rotational stuff to see if we need to intervene with therapy, for example. It is a complex map on what we do, why we do it, and how we do it. It is not just a box to check since everyone does med balls.

MB: I've often had Bondarchuk tell me to ease off releases or other special strength work before. He'll say, "Take it easy; you have the throws in the ring to throw hard." These exercises were just to put in some volume and emphasize the movements.

PFAFF: I really think the parasympathetic/sympathetic response thing is a factor. After my athletes go through our medicine ball circuits six or seven times, it becomes flow state. They don't have to do a lot of thinking. When we look at heart rate rhythms, the rates are very high, up to 160 or 170 with some kids. Later on, the rates are in the 50s for some athletes. I don't understand all the newest heart rate stuff or the variability stuff, but if your heart rate starts at 150 and later it is 50, something is happening, and we are attacking some parts of the autonomic nervous system for sure.

MB: You mentioned density earlier, and your approach to peaking is quite interesting since you often leave volume and intensity high, but drop the density. From my understanding you are like Bondarchuk in thinking that there is an important role for training at 100% so that technique is tested under stress.

PFAFF: That leads us to a catch phrase that creates havoc. It's called work capacity. To me work capacity is very, very, very specific. There is a myth out there that if you do a lot of anaerobic work or if you have an aerobic base that your work capacity improves in all entities. If you are going to throw 8-kilogram hammers, it takes you a while to get the volume up. The work capacities you need enzymatically, mitochondrial enzymes, nerve systems, pollution control, are specific to an 8-kilogram hammer. Doing cardio on the treadmill will not help you do more 8-kilogram throws. There is a misunderstanding about what work capacity is.

Every entity has a movement screen, and each has its own unique work capacity. Through time you want to see that improve. And, you realize that in some cases, there is a ceiling due to physiology where work capacity just stops. For example, I mentioned the maximum speed runs have a ceiling of six. You can do more and more lactic work, more weight training, more Olympic lifting, but after six absolute speed runs, people start to decline. We don't have the technology yet to know why. Some genetically gifted athletes can do up to nine. Back in the steroid and EPO days, there were people that could do 12-15, but we don't see those numbers now that testing has caught up.

IN-SEASON TRAINING: THE THREE-DAY ROLLOVER PLAN

MB: **I referred to your approach to peaking, earlier, and you are well known for the "three-day rollover" training plan you use in season. Essentially, you strip training down to its basics. For sprinters, that means you rotate through three workouts focused on the three main elements of sprinting: acceleration, max speed, and speed endurance. I like the beauty in the simplicity here, and I am wondering how you came to start using this approach.**

PFAFF: I've always coached a lot of disciplines at various levels. Back in the 1980s there were a lot more competitive opportunities at various levels in Europe. The German circuit had 30-40 meets, another dozen in Italy, ten in Spain; Sweden had a Grand Prix, etc. I had athletes at all levels from what is now the Diamond League to what we called the sausage circuit. I would have 30 athletes all over Europe and I would write exact programs for each one for the whole summer, and it never went according to plan. The weather might be bad and wipe out a meet; they may get into a meet

39

TRAINING TALK

at the last minute, and so on. And this was before internet, cell phones, and texts. We relied on calling cards and faxes, and it got to be insane to rewrite the program so often.

> **>> Contingency planning is a staple of great generals.**

Being a military history buff, contingency planning is a staple of great generals. Contingency-wise we were failing badly. Athletes were all over the place, and no one, consistently, had a good battle plan. So we looked at the essentials of each event: what are some of the key things we needed to do during the summer? That gave us some flexibility. I started to notice in programming trends that if you are into the essence of what is going on, a program should be able to shrink or expand and still have reliability and integrity. That was another litmus test we used on this.

MB: **We often hear about the three-day rollover in the context of sprinting, but you use it with all events. Now, you are focused on coaching the field events. How do you set up the three days there?**

PFAFF: Most field events, at least the jumps, you still have the sprint element. With the jumpers we will do an acceleration workout, a jump workout, and the day three workout will alternate between a speed workout and a lactic workout. The weight room is programmed to need. Some jumpers retain strength in season; some don't. A person that needs more of a top-off every seven to 10 days will have to get in the weight room and get after it. But you have to space out the other work and it comes at a cost.

With throwers, it was a little bit easier. We cycled the type of throwing workouts over the three days. One day was high quality, low volume. The second day was more technical refinement. And the third day was a volume day. The weight training reacted off those days. Physiologically, again, we look at whether they retain strength or lose elasticity. Some throwers have to amp the plyometric program a little more in season.

With jumpers, we have found that plyometric training is a good coordinative organizer for them. We have applied that to some throwers that have lost global coordination; a plyometric session somewhere in the three days would improve their overall coordination. We just use a loose template, and we can fine-tune that to the athlete and event.

> > *We just use a loose template, and we can fine-tune that to the athlete and event.*

MB: **And, you've found that this approach not only allows athletes to maintain during the competition season, but also reach a peak, correct?**

PFAFF: With the first athletes, I noticed that some of the people who often had to prioritize plyometric or power training were getting incredible marks at the end of the season. I was worried that the three-day might detrain these individuals over time, but some of them were actually improving.

More recently I had a Korean pole vaulter, Yoo Suk Kim, who came to me with a series of injuries and was so injured that he could not train like normal. So we started with the three-day rollover in the fall. We did a little more volume, but spread it out over three days of training a week so that, in between, we could do therapy and motor reeducation.

Asian athletes have a crazy competition schedule with meets from January to November. He wanted to do indoors, so we rolled that right into the indoor season and he had one of his best indoor seasons ever and that was off of an unconventional fall training. His federation only accepted world championship qualifiers from outdoor meets, so that put a priority on early outdoor meets like Mt. SAC in April. So after indoors we stayed

TRAINING TALK

on the three-day since there wasn't enough time to go back to work. He then hit the qualifier like three times in April and May.

After that, he went to Europe and he stayed on it. He tied his season's best at the World Championships in August and then, stayed on it for some of the Asian Championships in October and November. In September, he was getting personal bests in lifts, multiple jump tests, multi-throws and more. It's not like he was doing new stuff; he had a huge training age and sophisticated menu before we started with it. I was a little like, "Whoa, what's going on here?"

Most innovations have been forced upon me through unique situations, be it unique injuries, unique athletes, or a unique space and time. You come up with contingency plans to get to the next station. Sometimes if you study those contingency plans, you realize that these might be better than your original plan.

> **>> Most innovations have been forced upon me through unique situations.**

MB: **That is something I wanted to ask about since you've told me before that you used a similar approach with Greg Rutherford in his lead up to the London Olympics. He was injury prone, and you used the three-day rollover throughout the year. It produced a national record and Olympic gold. When we were talking about it, you said you were thinking about implementing it more broadly with athletes. Have you tried it with other athletes in a more standard situation? Or, have you thought further about it since then?**

PFAFF: Not yet, but I am leaning more towards it. We have a relationship with a genetics company. Two female pole vaulters I had got healthier and emotionally better whenever they went off to Europe in the summer.

Then, when they came back and we trained classically, the wheels came off the truck. In the genetic testing there is a block of eight genes we look at for recovery, and both of these girls were low in all eight genes. They just don't recover.

With those girls, we are more on a four-day cycle in the autumn and winter, mostly because psychologically, they cannot handle a three-day cycle. Their entire past, they have trained six days a week, often twice a day; to reduce them all the way to three days would be asking too much emotionally. So, we use four days and do warm-ups on the days in between, so that they think they are training, but it is more of an active recovery session.

MB: **Do you think that is a big reason why people don't consider these simple approaches as much as they should?**

PFAFF: The biggest hurdle for people in implementing the three-day plan, especially in season, is the addiction to work and the density of work. When you are young and try harder, you get better. But, there is a tipping point somewhere in your evolution where trying harder is the enemy. However, by that time you are addicted to trying harder, since in the first three years of your development trying hard was the magic answer.

>> **When you are young and try harder you get better, but there is a tipping point somewhere in your evolution where trying harder is the enemy.**

It is the same thing with training plans. There may have been a year where you trained your ass off, and the planets aligned. Maybe you did 12 sessions a week and had your golden year; then, you think that is the way you have to do it. I'd say that in most athlete interviews we have, we see that

TRAINING TALK

athletes are married to that golden year and can cite chapter and verse on what they did on each day.

Most world class athletes will also have a year where it doesn't go right because of injuries or something else, but they rallied it at the end of the year to turn things around for a great performance at the culminating meet. But, you ask them for details about that year, and they don't remember anything.

MB: **And that's more important to learn from. One big reason I am curious about this aspect of your training is that it looks very familiar to my approach and Bondarchuk's approach. He essentially trims training down to the basics, repeats it, then systematically changes the exercises used. And, we use that throughout the year.**

PFAFF: The reason this works, and Bondarchuk works for throwers, is because you are training in a conjugate fashion. You have a hierarchy of training qualities, prioritize that hierarchy, eliminate the esoteric, and embrace the power of density. That is why these systems work. Generally programming is too dense with too many training items. The more variables you have, you don't know what is producing change. With this and with Bondarchuk, the variables are reduced and you can start doing trend analysis to identify modulators. If the menu item list is five pages long, you cannot identify the modulators.

MB: **In the chat I recently had with Bondarchuk, he told me that one of the main benefits of his method isn't the method per se, but the fact that you can get a half dozen peaks a year and with each one you learn something. If you have just one peak a year, and you screw things up, you have lost a year. Screw things up again the next time, and two years are gone.**

Bondarchuk does not always get things right, but by having fewer variables and more peaks per year, he knows in a month or two if the plan worked and that helps him make the next plan better. It's just an improved trial and error system.

PFAFF: That goes back to the golden year. The golden year took place at a specific place and time, but years later, you are no longer there. If you get more slaps at peaking in your current state you get a more accurate answer on what works than looking at what happened a few years ago. Trend analysis is very time-sensitive and time-powered. If you use old data, you can glean some things, but it doesn't have the power of current data.

TRAINING PHILOSOPHIES

MB: **During one of your apprenticeship programs you said, "Many coaches have a very large toolbox but cannot decide what to do because they don't have a philosophy." How would you describe your philosophy?**

PFAFF: I think that training should be enjoyable, educational, and mechanical efficiency should drive the bus. The more mechanically efficient you are, the less injuries you will have, and that increases productivity. We strive for designing programs that allow you to learn and grow and be excited and find it interesting. They allow for accountability, transparency, and good communication, and that moves things forward from the mechanical efficiency standpoint. If it doesn't address those areas then why is it in there?

>> **One of the problems with current sport is that people have lost the concept of play and fun and why they are doing it.**

One of the problems with current sport is that people have lost the concept of play and fun and why they are doing it. I ask incoming athletes, "Why are you doing this?" They often answer, "What?" They never really think about it; they just get on the train and, before they know it, they are here.

MB: **I like that you mention fun first. That's why most of us starting doing sport but sometimes we lose sight of it and it is rarely discussed at coaching conferences.**

TRAINING TALK

PFAFF: I have a broad population of athletes every year, and there are always some athletes I cannot wait to get to because we have fun. I have some athletes that are in a bad spot or bad state of life; it is interesting with them, but not always fun. As a coach, you have to charge up to do those sessions. If you have to charge up for every athlete, every day, every week, you will burn out. Fun is the recharge.

MB: **How did you come to this philosophy? Has that always been your core philosophy or has it evolved over the last few decades?**

PFAFF: Mechanical efficiency has been there since day one. I think the enjoyment and fun paradigm came 30 years into coaching. I got burnt out, pissed off, tired of politics, fighting drug cheats, and started to ask myself why I got in this? I lost my compass and asked why I did sport as a kid: what attracted me to coaching? What were my best moments? The common thread was that it was fun and interesting.

MB: **That is the nice thing about working with younger athletes. I'd like to have more elite throwers in my group, but with beginners you are reminded every day why we do this. When they make their first breakthrough or throw a new best it's the best day of their life.**

PFAFF: Or they get a concept. I've had kids that have changed their sleep hygiene, and a lot of issues they were battling changed. When you see that light go on and they realized that something as simple and cheap as sleep changed their world, it is fun. It is not just about sport then, but about life. That's why I coach.

MB: **So you start with a philosophy and build off of it. How do you take the philosophy and turn it into a program or a plan?**

PFAFF: If you are into efficiency and it is one of your main drivers, then you are looking for metabolic efficiency, biomechanical efficiency, and efficiency on all fronts for the athlete and that event.

The underlying checklist against all you are doing should be:
- Is this efficient?
- Is there a more efficient way to do this?
- Is there a simpler, more repeatable, and reliable method?

The mountaintop of wisdom here is: let me have fewer variables so I can actually figure out what is driving that trend.

KEY PERFORMANCE INDICATORS & DEBRIEFING

MB: **I'd like to get an idea of how you approach an event, so let's take the hammer for example. How would you approach the event? How do you determine the training focus, and what do you think hammer throwers can learn from other events in this regard?**

PFAFF: Again, this goes back to our generation concept. I don't think I'd train a hammer thrower much different than other events. I would do a KPI analysis to determine what the KPIs are for that athlete at that stage of career development. I would prioritize those KPIs. The highest KPIs would get the most attention and density during the training week. The secondary KPIs would fill in the gaps. And all the work would be done with this movement screen idea, where you are constantly evaluating movement to adjust KPIs, prevent injury, and enhance skill.

I'd also go back to the parasympathetic/sympathetic concept. I've always been curious with range throwing, where guys throw in different zones. At those lower zones, is it really parasympathetic response? And what is it doing to the brain maps?

MB: **Is this something hammer throwers do better or worse than other events?**

PFAFF: I traffic in a lot of circles and have a lot of friends in the throws world. It is amazing to me that athletes and coaches don't do thorough debriefs after each competition or each training year or each cycle to an-

TRAINING TALK

alyze whether they accomplished what they were trying to accomplish. People have loose debriefs and loose target discussions about upcoming programs, but the plot gets lost and people default to comfort zones of training and emphasis.

For some reason I have been coaching a lot of pole vaulters over the last six or eight years. They might not do a speed endurance workout for two or three weeks, but when they come back to it they don't lose a step. It begs the question of how many hits of these various regimes do we really need in a given time frame?

There is a therapist of a world-class discus thrower who I share with a lot. He realized, at an advanced age, he probably didn't need to lift as much and as frequently, but after a rough start to the season he went back to what he did 10 years ago. When panic sets in, we tend to default to that magic year we had and stray away from the current KPIs and KPI intentions.

MB: **On the one hand you learn a lot about yourself over the years and what works. On the other hand, circumstances definitely do change.**

PFAFF: With this athlete, he has had multiple surgeries and injuries that have continued to manifest. The body and mind he is training with today is much different than what he had eight years ago.

MB: **Definitely. I'm at the point now where I want to do what I did years ago, but that is not necessarily what is best for me right now. It feels comfortable.**

PFAFF: One of the rages right now is about variability, anti-fragile, and this kind of stuff. A lot of times life presents the variables. You are a lawyer, working and writing; weather is crappy in Switzerland; you don't have your coach there. There is a lot of variability every day. Because there are new variances you have to have new KPIs and new plans.

I've also been asked many times in many interviews, "How does an advanced coach working with an advanced age athlete continue to excel?" I think it is this juggling game of KPIs. Both parties need to identify different generations of KPIs and learn to juggle throughout the year.

MB: **You are also well known for a business-like approach to analyzing competitions and seasons with your athletes. You sit down and have debriefings, for example, and set objectives. What are some of the things you are looking for in the debriefings?**

PFAFF: Most debriefs involve an understanding of where we are at. We are reverse engineering what we did in the meet, what was the warm up like, what was the self-talk, what was the day before, the previous meet, how did it all influence the performance? It could be the lifestyle, therapy inputs, the training, where you are in the stage of development. For some of the athletes, the debrief is lifestyle-centric because the lifestyle problems are an inhibitor. We look at the KPIs. That stands for not just key performance indicators, but also key performance inhibitors. The debrief is a constant tap dance around inhibitors and enhancers. By reviewing those things, you can ascertain if you are on the philosophical road or not.

In any industry, communication, transparency, and accountability are metric landmarks. How do you get better reporting and communication? It is through knowledge of what you are doing. It is through broad knowledge and deep knowledge. A sidebar of our philosophy is: be a student of what's going on.

MB: **I just did an interview with John Kiely, and this was an important point for him. He was basically saying that the future of periodization hinges on education of athletes. Better periodization will come through individualization. And that comes from better feedback. The way to get the best feedback is by becoming partners with the athletes; the more they understand, the better feedback they can give.**

TRAINING TALK

PFAFF: We fail to study and learn from industry too. Why do a lot of major companies go under after they have been alive 20 years? It's the communication of the entire organization breaking down. It is usually the blue-collar guys coming up with great new ideas or identifying problems, but if the dynamic isn't there, then you don't get that information. As a coach, you do not want your athlete silent and ignorant; you are stunting the process, and it will inevitably collapse. We don't study systems engineering in sports.

In the book *Good to Great: Why Some Companies Make the Leap...And Others Don't,* Jim Collins looks at companies that were blue chip over a long period of time versus flaming stars that cratered. You see a lot more horizontal in the long term than top-down leadership. My question, when I see a top-down organization or process, is, "What is the driver for success?" You need to know the longevity of that driver and if this driver is sustainable.

4 // GARY WINCKLER

Mastering biomechanics and the leading training methods is not enough to become one of the best sprint coaches in the world. In the highly competitive sport of sprinting, you need to be ahead of the curve. The task is simple: get from point A to point B the fastest, and coaches have tried out nearly every trick in the book. This describes Gary Winckler's path to the top.

Winckler not only mastered the basics of sprinting, but was one of the first coaches in North America to implement some of Frans Bosch's concepts and focus on topics like injury prevention. In 2008, he retired after 23 years as a coach at the University of Illinois. Prior to that he had spent time at Florida State University. Throughout his career he coached over 175 All-Americans and more than a dozen Olympians. Winckler's teams won 11 conference titles in the Big Ten, and he also took home 11 conference coach of the year honors. One year after retirement he was inducted into the US Track & Field and Cross Country Coaches Association Hall of Fame.

Winckler also has had success beyond the sprints. In fact his two most successful athletes were hurdlers: 2003 World Champion and Canadian 100-meter hurdles record holder Perdita Felicien and 1996 Olympic 400-meter hurdles bronze medalist Tonja Buford-Bailey. As of this printing, Buford-Bailey's personal best remains the fifth fastest of all-time.

TRAINING TALK

In retirement, he has turned his attention to his saddle-making company, but that doesn't mean Winckler's lost his touch. He continues to stay up to date on the sport, write, teach, and work as an athletics consultant. In our discussion in 2014, we covered reactivity training, periodization, training technique, and a variety of other topics.

LESSONS TO LEARN

- Training methods influence technique. If you want to preserve or improve technique, training loads need to allow for quality technical movements. And if the technical element is missing from a block of training, it is difficult to connect what you are working on back to your event. For example, a block of maximum strength work will get you strong, but if technical work is absent it is hard to make sure that the strength gains can be applied on the track.

- When training technique, each part is connected. Many technical problems in clearing the hurdle can be fixed by working on the takeoff, just as problems with the release of a throw can be fixed by correcting the beginning. Similarly, properly preparing a movement can generate more force using the reactive training principles described by Frans Bosch.

- Finding the technical model for your athlete should be an individualized approach. Posture is simply about finding the best position to apply force, and technique is the same. As individuals have different levels of speed, strength, and size, those positions might vary. Following what others do without a critical analysis is a recipe for disaster.

REACTIVITY TRAINING

MB: **You may be best known as a hurdle coach, but you have also coached a lot of other events. Which events have you worked with?**

WINCKLER: I didn't start in the sport myself until I was a junior in high school. We didn't have a track program until my junior year. I ran hurdles a little, but I was primarily a high jumper, long jumper, and triple jumper. It was the same throughout college. When I went to graduate school at Oregon State I was helping Will Stevens with the jumpers there too. When I went to Florida State I inherited some sprinters and hurdlers and I had to learn to be a sprint coach. That is how it's been.

People get labeled as a certain type of coach, but if you are fortunate in your recruiting or inherit some athletes you have to become a hurdle coach to survive. I've coached every event: cross country, steeplechase, a few pole vaulters, and throwers. When I was a head coach in college I would typically pick up the events where our coaches didn't have as much experience.

MB: **I'm sure that gives you some perspective to compare and contrast training among different event groups. This is a broad question, but what can track events learn from each other? For example, what do you see in hurdle training that throwers or jumpers might be overlooking?**

WINCKLER: I actually had the chance to coach the hammer back in 2007 and asked myself the same thing. What I was trying to do was apply some of the reactivity principles that Frans Bosch talks about. As the turns get quicker, the speed of contact with the ground gets quicker. I was trying to coach the angle and reactivity on the ground. This is the same thing I was trying to do with hurdlers in their take off. It would have been fun to continue to do it for a few more years. It seemed to make sense for me.

MB: **Could you explain a little more about the concept for those that might not be as familiar with Bosch's work?**

TRAINING TALK

WINCKLER: The concept is that we sprint primarily through the production of vertical forces. The best sprinters are those that put the most amount of force into the ground in the least amount of time. When you get above 7.5 meters/second in your running, the only way to produce forces in that short amount of time is to produce them reactively. And so, we set up the body to allow the tendons such as the Achilles and IT band, the elastic anatomical components in the body, to produce force because they are the only things that can produce forces that high at that speed.

In sprinting, people have talked about the ankle for a long time and how it needs to be a rigid structure when it contacts the ground to take slack out of the system. If the ankle is rigid when you hit the ground, you will be rigid in the knee and hip as well and you'll have a solid system where the muscles are all tense and allow the tendons to stretch and reflex, which will give high forces in a short amount of time.

To take it a step further, if you just try to keep the ankle rigid when the foot contacts the ground the ankle will always collapse. Once the ankle collapses, the knee and hip will collapse as well. So you've lost the rigidity in the system. Frans would say there is slack introduced into the system. What has to occur is that just prior to the foot coming in contact with the ground—for the purposes of conversation let's say about one centimeter off the ground—the foot needs to actively plantar flex into the ground. The active plantar flexion shortens the system and gives it a greater potential for rigidity, and you don't have the collapsing occur.

MB: **How did you implement the reactivity principles in hurdles and hammer throw?**

WINCKLER: So in hurdling, I would utilize this on the penultimate step before the hurdle. If we can get this kind of reactivity off the ground on the penultimate step, it ultimately then makes the action of the lead leg automatic and transfer the momentum from the run between the hurdles to the takeoff and clearance of the next hurdle.

That was my initial goal, but once I started playing with this, I was surprised how easily athletes pick it up and also discovered that the quality of reactivity off of the penultimate step ultimately determined the quality of the flight over the hurdle. So, if we had situations where arms were going off to the side or the lead leg was coming across the middle of the body (situations people often try to correct while the athlete is in the air) if you simply went back and corrected what was going on in the last two steps before the hurdle to achieve a good reactive force production then all the anomalies over the hurdle disappeared. It made coaching the event very easy. This make sense since if you are coaching the long jump or high jump and don't like the flight, what do you do? You go back and look at what happened on the ground.

We tried the same thing in the hammer. As the right foot came down they would be more reactive with the ankle in the ways I described earlier. In other words, have the toe up, and as the foot comes to the ground, be very active with the plantar flexion to speed up the right hip.

The important concept of all of this in throwing, sprinting, or any activity you are going to do this reactive work with, is that the foot has to enter perpendicular to the ground. Everything is down from above. When the right foot comes around in the hammer, it comes down from above, performs the reaction off of the ground, and, boom, accelerates the hip around.

MB: **I find the impact on technique very interesting, and I'll get back to that point later, but I'm curious whether the reactive element is trained as a technical point through cues or is it acquired through supplemental exercises in the weight room?**

WINCKLER: I try to incorporate it into some of the weight room activity we do. I pretty much put together my training in a very thematic way. If the theme of the day is speed, it doesn't mean we can't go to the weight room or do longer running, it just means that every activity we do that

TRAINING TALK

day will be addressing speed. So if we are doing flying 30-meter runs or technical work on the track, we might end the session by going into the weight room and doing snatches or reactive step ups, where the goal is not necessarily moving a lot of weight but it's about working coordination with a resistance.

MB: **Bondarchuk classifies exercises into four categories on a scale of specificity. The competitive exercise is the most specific and after that are specific developmental exercises (what most people call specific strength or special strength exercises). They essentially develop strength by overloading part of the movement. Some of those exercises sound like they would fall into that category. What are some other exercises that hurdlers might use to develop parts of the movement?**

WINCKLER: Whenever I have athletes hurdle, we hurdle over the whole hurdle. We don't do lead leg or trail leg exercises because I think they detract from the coordination of the entire movement. We will do short approach runs or standing approach runs on a long jump runway and perform the takeoff mechanism into a sand pit. There is no hurdle there but we are working on the timing of the penultimate foot and the quick scissoring action following that foot contact into the takeoff foot.

>> *Whenever I have athletes hurdle, we hurdle over the whole hurdle. We don't do lead or trail leg exercises because I think they detract from the coordination of the entire movement.*

We will do some resistance exercises with a harness. The athlete is either in place or gradually moving down the track working on foot reactivity and quick leg exchange. Those are pretty key elements in the reactive strength production concepts.

It is similar to throwers: we will take partial movements and strengthen them. We don't use a lot of exercises since the ones I use can be fairly complex in nature, in terms of their coordination and timing. The goal each time we do them is to just do them a little better.

We will also do bouncing movements on the track with one or two feet working on the timing of the foot. The way I use those exercises is as a progression. If the basic one is performed well, we will move onto the next after a few reps. It is more based on learning, rather than any kind of conditioning.

PERIODIZATION & ANNUAL PLANNING

MB: **In an interview you did with the Canadian Athletics Coaching Centre a few years ago, you mentioned that you started your career using a more standard periodization approach that cycled volume and intensity in the model of Leo Matveyev. Over the course of your career, you stopped doing that. You also started to make sure you are working on all elements of training throughout the year, rather than proceeding through phases. What led you to make that transition?**

WINCKLER: Because the Matveyev model just simply doesn't work, particularly in speed and power events. If you try to apply that model in a practical setting, you will get a point, and it's usually when the volume and intensity curves cross, where things will blow up.

>> *The Matveyev model just doesn't work.*

If you look at the reality of most speed and power events, the volume of training doesn't change too much throughout the course of the year, and the intensity doesn't change that much either. If you are training speed and power, you need to be training qualitative movements, and if you are training qualitative movements, there has to be the element of speed in

57

TRAINING TALK

the movement at all times. There will be fluctuations in volume and loading of course, but to me it is more of a wave curve that goes up and down throughout the course of the year.

The longer I've been a coach, the more I've realized that the training has to really positively influence your technical model. Some of the older models I used to follow, you'd do a four-week cycle focusing on maximal strength. The problem you find when you focus on maximal strength for a four week period, is that you will improve your maximal strength qualities, but what you're not doing is improving the athlete's ability to adapt that maximal strength to performance. We found that coming out of cycles like that you are slower and less coordinated in technical movements so that maximal strength really didn't give us any boost to our performance. Whereas if I blend the maximal strength work in with other work as we went along, over the long term we are constantly adapting the gains in strength into performance.

MB: **I see the same thing in the throws. Throwers enter heavy lifting phases in the fall, and their bodies are so beat up that they can't get into the positions needed in the throw. They compensate with bad habits that take longer to fix, but maybe I'm biased since that isn't Bondarchuk's approach.**

WINCKLER: I think there are a lot of similarities between what we are doing. One of the things I think I do similarly is making training performance-based. What we are doing has to ultimately contribute to performance. When I speak with coaches, I am really big on this. They always want to turn the conversation to how much of this activity do you do. I keep trying to bring it back to the fact that no matter what you do, make sure it is contributing to the end goal. It is not always about the exercises. You may have the right exercises, but you may not be having the athlete perform the exercise correctly.

MB: **You were also saying that you work on all components of training throughout the year. When I hear many sprint coaches talk, they will** often start with longer distances to build a speed-endurance base, then work down to shorter distances throughout the year. Or they will build speed over shorter distances and, then, try to extend that throughout the year wrote about. How do you look at that debate through the lens of doing all components at once?

WINCKLER: It is kind of a combination of the two. Our situation determined that we had to do some combinations. Ideally I would like to work more short-to-long to preserve the quality of running and make sure they can maintain the quality as the distance progresses to longer distances. At the same time you have to be ready for indoor season on the 1st of January and after mid-November the weather forced our training inside too. Then, you have to have certain capacities and levels of fitness that you have to achieve maybe through hill running or longer-type speed endurance. One day we might do longer hill runs, another shorter speed work. It wasn't ideal but we were able to get the job done that way.

Quality was the theme throughout though. If you are going to try and preserve the quality of movement and ingrain movement patterns, contributing to positive change in performance in any speed and power event, then you have to be able to prescribe volumes of work and exercises so that the athlete is going to be able to maintain quality of movements.

I always give the example of giving a speed endurance workout of five x 200 meters and the athlete can only do three with good running quality. Yet, they still do all five, and the last two look like shit. What have you done? You have basically taken 40% of the workout and destroyed the good things that you tried to gain with the other 60% of the workout. What have you gained? Nothing, in my opinion.

We have to be smart about how we do this. If we really want to encourage the athlete to run correctly all the time we have to prescribe volumes that they can perform to a certain point that the technique breaks down

TRAINING TALK

and, then, we either stop, change the activity, or shorten the distance to maintain the quality.

That is where I have been the last four or five years of my coaching. It is not an easy sale. Most people would say you have to run a certain volume. But if it is always two steps forward one step back then you are using a greater volume of work than you need to get where you need to go.

MB: **Another question about the yearly plan: You are good at peaking your athletes when it counts, which is easier said than done. What is your peaking philosophy? Does your training change a lot as you get close to the big meets?**

WINCKLER: A little bit; we will gradually drop off the volume of work we do, but to me the peaking process is more about understanding early on in the year what the demands of the situation are going to be at that major competition. Is it going to be three or four rounds? Will you have to run three or four days in a row like at NCAAs? The better understanding a coach has of those demands at the end of the year, the sooner you can start adapting the athlete to those demands. If I have a good sprinter that will have to run hard several days in a row, I will have some micro-cycles back in January through March where we will work hard for four days in a row.

The other key aspect to peaking is that as you get into the last three weeks before the competition you are not changing exercises. You are only using exercises you have well-established patterns in. Nothing new. I do not want any adaptation occurring at this point. I just want refinement. We will come out and do some of the same routines and workouts, just seeking better timing and execution of those exercises.

MB: **There is no big taper then?**

WINCKLER: No. But, then again, there is individualization. You have to understand the athletes as well. For that reason, we will practice tapering earlier in the year to see how they adapt. With some athletes, if you take away too much volume, they go in the crapper right away. They need that workload. They need to be in the weight room. Maybe not as much, but they need to do that work. With others, you can take away a lot more work, and they blossom and look even better, as the workloads decrease. You can have your principles you want to follow, but there is still individualization of how athletes adapt.

> >> With some athletes, if you take away too much volume they go in the crapper right away. They need that workload.

The athlete also has to like what they are doing. Another reason not to change the exercises in the late period is so the athlete feels confidence by doing it better. Sometimes you take away routines too much and athletes lose confidence since they feel like they are not working. Psychologically, they feel that they are not ready.

I'll take the example of Bershawn Jackson getting ready for the 2009 World Championships. He always liked to run 500-meter runs; they were a constant he had grown up with and always liked to do. We were in training camp in Germany a couple days out from the meet, and he wants to do a couple of 500s so we did them. They were good quality; he came through 400 in 46.0. That's what we did since that's what he needed to psychologically feel he was ready.

COACHING TECHNIQUE AND POSTURE

MB: Another thing you mentioned in the Canadian Athletics Coaching Centre interview is that posture plays a big role in your approach to coaching and training. It sounds simple, but how exactly do you implement that?

TRAINING TALK

WINCKLER: Posture is a result of force application. With runners, I look at what happens when the foot hits the ground. You can apply this to throwers as well. If I want to change someone's posture I look at where the foot is with respect to their center of mass. Then, I look at the quality of force application coming from the foot. If that is proper and under the hips, I will have a tall posture. If I am accelerating from the blocks and the force application is on the ground longer and pushing behind me, I will have a natural lean forward. That doesn't mean it is a poor posture, just that it is a good posture for that activity.

Posture is just a result of where the foot is with respect to the center of mass and the quality of force application. For me, it is as simple as that. When you see a lot of the male sprinters today running down the track trying to hold their bodies low for 60 meters, that's an artificial posture.

MB: **So what you are focusing on is applying force correctly, and, if you do that, the posture will follow.**

WINCKLER: Exactly. The concept most coaches have for coming out of the blocks is horizontal force application. If your focus is horizontal force application you will see athletes stumble and overstride early on in the acceleration phase, and they will struggle to get to a tall posture for maximum velocity later. Whereas, if you have an athlete coming out of the blocks and tell them to push up off the ground, in other words create a vertical force, that will automatically change their posture and get them the maximum velocity, when it needs to be there. It is another one of those really simple concepts that self-corrects what the body is supposed to be doing. You don't have to think about a transition or that you need to be at maximum velocity at 30 meters. Your body will come to maximum velocity when it is ready to; it might be at 28 meters or 35 meters, and that will change as your fitness changes throughout the course of the year.

MB: **Again, it comes back to focusing on the basics. Earlier you mentioned that when you fix a problem in the takeoff mechanism, it will fix** the movement over the hurdle. The same thing happens in the throwing events. For example, fixing basic problems out of the back of the ring in the shot put can clean up the release. Are there any times when you are actively coaching something that happens in the air?

WINCKLER: The only thing I will sometimes talk about in the air is that some athletes have the habit of pointing their trail leg toe downward after taking off, rather than turning it to the outside. You see this in particular with some taller females that can clear the hurdle by eight inches, so they don't have to pull their trail foot in the correct position. The only thing I will tell them is to invert the foot and point the toe to the side.

Since I have been working with these reactivity concepts in the last two steps, generally speaking I don't find myself coaching anything in the air at all. The typical reaction you get from an athlete, when they perform it well for the first time is that they come off of the hurdle on the other side and stumble. They wonder what happened and what happened, is they performed the takeoff so well that they preserved velocity and are through the hurdle and on the ground before they are ready to be on the ground. So, it catches them by surprise.

MB: **You see this in the throws too. Someone does something right, but then, throws into the cage since it puts them in the unfamiliar position of having a long time to accelerate the implement.**

I actually see quite a few similarities between the hammer, in particular, and the hurdles. Both are quite rhythmic events. A shot putter does their movement just once in the throw. But in the hammer, we take the same movement—a turn—and repeat it three or four times. In the hurdles, you are taking the same element—clearing a hurdle—and repeating it. The hammer is cyclical and rhythmic.

In the hurdles are you actively coaching rhythm? Are you coaching each hurdle or the entire race?

TRAINING TALK

WINCKLER: Really, the entire race. We do two basic sessions with hurdlers. One session a week is focused on the takeoff mechanism and hurdle clearance. The other is called rhythm endurance work where we are working to increase and maintain the rhythm of the run. Those runs will be anywhere from seven to 12 hurdles in length. The concept we want is the same as a sprinter. If the sprinter is thinking about accelerating in a 100-meter race up to 50 or 60 meters, we want the hurdlers to feel like they can accelerate through five or six hurdles.

It is all about frequency: 90% of the people will take the same number of steps throughout the race so it is about who can do it faster. We work a lot with discounted hurdle spacing in training because that tends to replicate the adrenaline effect you get in racing, in terms of the hurdles coming up faster and the step frequency being faster, but you always must maintain your takeoff distance. That is the biggest mistake that occurs with elite hurdlers is that they overrun hurdles and are too close to the hurdle and lose that takeoff distance. As soon as they do that, they decelerate. They have to.

MB: **I have read some about the question of whether to use seven or eight steps before the first hurdle. Last year Brooks Johnson wrote about why he switched David Oliver to seven steps. You have used eight with your women. What are your thoughts on the topic?**

WINCKLER: Well it takes a pretty special athlete to do seven steps. You see more men do it than women. I don't like it with women since the step length in seven steps is too different from the step lengths you will use between the hurdles. I want this rhythm to be building from the blocks up through the first five hurdles.

To make seven steps work, a female athlete will have to drive a lot longer and make their first seven steps longer than they will utilize between the hurdles. So, there is a sudden change of rhythm there. They are better off staying with eight steps to carry that faster rhythm into the runs between the hurdles. The same with the men.

I consulted with Tonja Buford-Bailey on changing Andrew Riley to seven steps in 2012, but he is a guy who can run under 10.2 in the 100 meters. He won the NCAA title in both the 100- and 110-meter hurdles. A lot of the guys I see today are not that powerful. Most of them are reaching and over striding in the last two steps to the hurdle to get there. It is not for everybody. Too many coaches are doing a wholesale switch right now, but when you look at these guys they are not ready to take seven steps.

MB: **The way you describe the pros and cons of each sounds very similar to how one would describe the pros and cons of using three versus four turns in the hammer throw. Neither one is right, but I find it interesting to hear the reasoning behind why an athlete chose one or the other.**

WINCKLER: Most of it is just groupthink. After Andrew won the NCAAs doing seven steps, it was amazing how many guys were out there doing seven steps. Just because he did it, they figured they had to. There is not always a lot of analytic thinking going on when these decisions are made.

That is what has always made coaching interesting, adapting the event to the individual. You start to find out what certain people's qualities are. When I was coaching the hammer throw, I only had a few throwers, and one was a 61- to 62-meter thrower from Sweden who couldn't handle the speed with four turns and was much better with three solid turns. If you get three good turns versus four mediocre turns, what is better?

TECHNOLOGY & COACHING

MB: **When it comes to coaching, are you more hands on, or are you using more technology like video review in training?**

WINCKLER: I would usually try to video technical work like the rhythm work I described. We would try to videotape those rhythm sessions, since it would allow me to accurately look at the touchdowns and look at the acceleration progressions throughout the runs and pick up some things that I couldn't always pick up with the naked eye. It is not that I couldn't

TRAINING TALK

pick it up with the naked eye, but typically when I do rhythm work, it's in a competitive situation with two or three hurdlers on the track at the same time, and the whole idea is that you're going to race each other. That way we can achieve faster rhythms. I can't watch everybody at the same time, so we would videotape it.

MB: **Are you watching the video in slow motion or real time? I ask because I find it a difficult balance: frame-by-frame shows you more detail but you lose the rhythm aspect.**

WINCKLER: We will watch it in real time for the purposes of getting the touchdown times. But we also watch in slow motion to look at the quality of the takeoff mechanism.

When I was working with the Canadians, I did not have to do a lot of video myself at training camps since we had a biomechanist who would do that for us. But we had videos placed in a stationary position to look at the three meters before the hurdle and look at the quality of the takeoff mechanism. That's all I ever looked at. If I see the right thing there I don't worry about what's happening over the hurdle, since it'll be OK.

Video can help, but it can be a curse too. When I started coaching, the only video you had was a 16-millimeter or 8-millimeter camera. You had to send that film off to be processed and maybe a week later you'd get it back. You had to learn to use your naked eye. In working with some young coaches the last couple of years, I keep telling them they are videoing too much because you're not allowing your eye to develop. You are too dependent on being able to go back and look at the video later.

It's a skill you can develop. If you know what you are looking for and you've looked at it thousands of time, you can look at a guy running down the track and know what's going on with him. That is a skill we should all try to develop as coaches. A video can be a nice supporting feature, but I don't take too much of it.

5 // PAT CONNOLLY

For a generation of athletes, Evelyn Ashford was the definition of speed. She ensured her legacy would last by winning double gold in front of a home crowd at the 1984 Olympics. By her side the whole way was her coach, Pat Connolly. Connolly began working with Ashford at age 18, first helping her qualify for the 1976 Olympics at age 19. Nearly a decade later, the whole world was chasing Ashford as she was able to improve season after season and set multiple world records along the way.

I got to know Connolly through her husband, Harold. Connolly was certainly the best coach in their family, as well as a three-time Olympian, finishing as high as sixth in the pentathlon at the 1968 Olympics. Harold, on the other hand, was the best athlete in the family. He was the last American to win gold in the hammer throw and held the world record for nearly a decade. When Harold retired from throwing, he continued as a coach, mentor, and strong advocate for the hammer throw until his untimely death in 2010.

After we first met in 2001, he helped coach me from afar, and remains one of my greatest mentors and inspirations. In working with Harold I quickly saw the mindset that took him to the top. He started the sport late with a significant physical disadvantage, yet overcame the odds to reach the top of his sport for more than a decade. To do that, he had to find his own way.

TRAINING TALK

Connolly overcame a lot to be among the world's best sprint coaches. Coaching remains a male-dominated profession and was even more so in the 1970s and 1980s, as women's sports were just beginning to grow. Connolly was at the forefront of women's collegiate sports, helping start UCLA's women's cross country and track and field teams and leading them to national titles in 1975 and 1977. Though she faced resistance from every direction, this is also where her success began in coaching a young sprinter named Evelyn Ashford, eight years before her glory in Los Angeles. Entering the sport at that time limited Connolly's opportunities, but it also freed her to think outside the box. Thus, while her philosophy is similar to many coaches, her methods are quite different, and certainly not the standard approach to training speed.

Later in her career, Connolly coached collegiately again, worked with professional athletes such as Renaldo Nehemiah, and guided an 18-year-old Allyson Felix to an Olympic silver medal in Athens, in addition to finding time to raise a family of her own.

In this interview, she outlines her general training philosophy, the role of specificity in training, the mental side of training, differences between coaching men and women, and more.

LESSONS TO LEARN

- Specificity is at the center of everything. It's a simple question, but always ask if what you are doing is specific to your event.

- Injury prevention is just as important as specificity. If you are injured, you cannot do any specific work.

- Repetition is the key. The mind-blowing volumes amassed by Connolly's athletes underscore its importance. Repeat something over and over with quality, and you will reach mastery.

GENERAL TRAINING PHILOSOPHY

MB: The most successful athlete you have worked with was Evelyn Ashford. When looking over the meet records for Weltklasse Zürich last summer I saw that the world record she ran there in 1984 still stands as the meet record 31 years later. We've made advances in track technology, footwear, biomechanics, and many other areas. Yet, a few decades later, sprinters are still not running as fast and throwers are not throwing as far. Do you think we are over-thinking our approach to training?

CONNOLLY: First of all, Evelyn was an amazing talent, but I was also a coach that was out of the box. During the 1960s I had exposure to the best coaches from Bill Bowerman to Gabriel Korobkov, the head coach of the Soviet Union. More importantly, I also had my own athletic experience and background as a woman that gave me insights into working with women. Tom Tellez was the major men's field events coach at UCLA when I started coaching Evelyn. He was always telling me I needed to change this or that, but I just said no. Women are different and still are.

The overarching factor on women's performances since then has been drugs. And it makes me crazy because there is no way to prove Evelyn's astounding achievements were made without the use of performance-enhancing drugs. For Evelyn to defeat the East Germans and to set world records, I had to get into her head by developing trust: that I would never lie or give her phony times like other coaches and that I would never ask her to do something of which she was not capable. I told her that the East Germans needed drugs and she didn't.

MB: **How would you describe your training philosophy in a few sentences?**

CONNOLLY: I always ask the question: is this specific to the event? And if not, is it essential to injury prevention? The rest of it you don't need.

Now specificity for throwers and sprinters includes things like plyometrics. Even though it is not specific to the technique, it is specific to fast-

TRAINING TALK

twitch muscular work. So while Evelyn lifted very little weight, she never did squats or snatches, she did plyometrics and countless fast tempo drills called shake-ups.

> >> I always ask the question: Is this specific to the event? And, if not, is it essential to injury prevention? The rest of it you don't need.

I've learned a lot, even since coaching Allyson Felix in 2004. I question every aspect of the workout. The injury prevention stuff has to be done every day throughout the season, but we don't waste time with unnecessary drills that aren't specific to the event, whether it is sprints or throws.

MB: You brought up the connection between sprints and throws there. You personally have a deep connection to the throws, not just through Harold, but as a pentathlete and three-time Olympian. When we have spoken previously, you've mentioned that you took some things from throwing and applied them to sprinting, and vice versa. I find those connections interesting; they are universal truths. What do you see as important links between the events?

CONNOLLY: The common thing that works is mental focus. The ability to focus and zone in and stay in the zone is the same across all sports and all events. It doesn't matter what type of technician you are or how much weight you lift. Being able to stay in that zone is what matters.

My favorite hammer thrower to watch was Litvinov, but my favorite hammer thrower was Kevin McMahon. What drew me to him was that he was the hammer throw, even more than Harold. Harold was always over-thinking everything, but Kevin was like a ballet dancer. It was in the movement and the feeling. Kevin was an artist with focus. That's the secret to sprinting and throwing and everything. Like Kevin, Evelyn had the ability to focus; she was hungry, and she wanted to do it. She once said that running at full speed is better than sex.

SPECIFICITY & INJURY PREVENTION

MB: **You mentioned that training must be either specific or help with injury prevention. Can you give some examples that help with injury prevention?**

CONNOLLY: Almost 90% of what I did as a coach was injury prevention. The actual technique and kinesthetic awareness required for sprinters to run at a speed faster than anyone has run before is scary. You can't sprint if you are injured. Injuries are a real part of the game, so I focused on prevention.

As a result of that, when I was coaching at Radford University the throwers were especially upset with me because I made them go on long walks like Allyson Felix had done. Because of the way your foot strikes in front and pulls your hips over your foot, you are developing butt power. Walking fast uphill requires even more development of butt power and also, strengthens the anterior tibialis, which is good for preventing shin splints.

>> *You cannot sprint if you are injured.*

My last coaching gig was at a boys' high school in Maryland, where I had a lot of football players. They came off the football program beat up and vulnerable to injuries. For their warm up, instead of jogging a mile, which was what the head coach had them do, I had them walk a half-mile as fast as they could. They hated it, as did the heavy throwers because it is hard; everyone was surprised how hard walking is. Injury prevention is the real secret of sprinting. All the other drills don't matter if you are hurt.

MB: **Back to the specific category, you've worked with many events and had to define what is specific for each of them. Do you see any connec-**

TRAINING TALK

tions there between different events or lessons learned on how to approach specificity?

CONNOLLY: When I was a pentathlete and I had to do everything from sprinting to shot putting. Before the spin was introduced, I hated the technique of shot putting and made up my own that I actually used in the 1968 Olympics. But the idea of standing stationary and hopping back and keeping momentum going was difficult for me. A common drill at the time was hop-backs, and it really worked my butt. Once I made that connection, I made it an instrumental part of my sprinters' training. You lean forward, stand on one leg, and hop back 10 times then repeat on the other leg.

MB: **Are there any more comparisons you see in approaching specific training for the different events?**

CONNOLLY: I had learned, at the end of my own career, a technique called shake-ups. The reason I am telling you is not because they will directly apply to throwers, but indirectly. Shake-ups are a way to have as many possible repetitions. You know, the more turns you can take, the more you get the feeling of it; it's the same with running. The more you can run at a fast tempo the better off you are.

Shake-ups are run barefoot on the grass as a form of low impact sprinting. When I started with Evelyn in the 1970s, we did shake-ups and she eventually was able to get up to 100 x 100 meters. They were done in sets of five with 15-20 seconds rest at the turn around to run back. After the fifth 100 meters they could walk 100 meters. We took water breaks from time to time, but that's 10 kilometers of speed work in one workout and it clearly led to her world record performances.

In fact, before the Olympics, in May 1984, we were doing that workout with some of my other athletes at UCLA. Joan Benoit Samuelson, who went on to win gold at the first Olympic women's marathon, came out to train. She did her whole workout and was getting ready to leave while Evelyn was running shake-ups. Joan said "What is this? I run for two and a half hours; you run for 11 seconds, but your workout is taking longer than mine." The point was to get speed, strength and stamina. In a sprint, who slows down the least at the end of the race wins, especially in the 200 meters.

Where that applies to throwing is in the number of repetitions. Harold was catching on to this principle later when he focused on turning and turning and turning. You need to focus on very specific repetition. Especially with high school athletes, they don't have time to do all the stuff professional athletes have come up with. Now there seems to be a speed coach on every high school campus and football team. There are endless amounts of drills they do, but what works and what is important, in the time that is available for each athlete, is to weed out the things you don't need to do.

MB: **What I remember the most from when Harold worked with me were those turns. My parents even poured a concrete slab in our backyard so I could do endless turns.**

CONNOLLY: Evelyn did not spend much time in the weight room, but she was a strong runner. What made Evelyn strong was that 10 kilometers of speed work on the grass. I was really glad when Harold got into using so many turns in his final years.

My background started as a kid in ballet. I danced a lot and learned much of my philosophy and developed an eye for movement from ballet. One of the terms I was told was that you haven't worked until you have reached your "seventh sweat." Ballet dancers aren't measured. They do not have to jump far or high; they have to jump so they look right, but they will work seven or eight hours a day on that.

The seventh sweat is about repetition. When you first start out you break a sweat, but you keep going and it will dry up. Then it happens again when you work a little harder. When you reach the seventh sweat you are

TRAINING TALK

exhausted and it is time to quit. That is a philosophy I did not put into practice, but it is the idea of repetition: doing something over and over until you become one with the event; until you are the swan in the lake.

> **>> [I]t is the idea of repetition: doing something over and over until you become one with the event; until you are the swan in the lake.**

MB: **In working with Bondarchuk, the philosophy is very similar, although he is focused more on the volume of throws than turns. The key is that you need to repeat what you want to be good at. Strength is more about how far you throw the 10-kilogram hammer or run 10 kilometers of grass sprints than it is how much you lift in the weight room. Leg power is also very important, which is specific in that it is an important factor in sprinting and throwing. You used a lot of plyometrics to train this. Can you give some examples of how you applied plyometrics in training for sprinters?**

CONNOLLY: The plyometric part is when you jump back down—the eccentric muscle contractions—that activate the fast-twitch fibers. So we did a lot of jumping. Bounding was in every workout and box jumps twice a week. Throwers should do the same.

Skipping is also totally under used and underrated. It requires strong feet and if you do it barefoot on grass you are using every single muscle in your foot and calves. You don't even have to pick your knees up. It is about the force you exert down on the ground that determines how fast you run or how far you throw.

We also used stairs a lot too. At UCLA's Drake Stadium there are 80 stairs going up, evenly spaced. My sprinters would run every single stair, and

I would time them, since that made them move their feet fast. There are only two factors that determine your time over 100 meters: stride length and stride rate. As you get stronger, your stride length increases naturally. Therefore I spent more time working on stride rate and with stairs the foot hits the ground sooner. There are 15 aisles in the stadium and we worked until we could do "15 ups." On our way to the Olympic Trials in Sacramento in 2004, Allyson, her brother Wes, and I stopped at UCLA to do a workout on those stairs. Other coaches criticized us for doing those stadium stairs so close to the Trials but she ran a new best at the Trials and won.

Throwers would do them too. They wouldn't have to do 15 x 80 stairs, but they would benefit from the foot power and keeping feet low to the ground and not picking up the knees. Tap, tap, tap, tap: it gets the rhythm ingrained. Then when you go into the circle, the kinesthetic awareness of that tempo will speed up things.

MB: **You cite skipping as great for the feet. Harold had mentioned to me that you also did a lot of work with sand to strengthen the feet too.**

CONNOLLY: Whenever we had sand, we trained in sand once a week. It is good cross training because it is great for total body fitness early in the season. However, I don't use it in the season. It gets your legs in shape, and it is better when you do it in the sand than on the hard ground. Sand was important to conditioning and cross training, but not so much to technique.

Athletes need variety. At the beach, you work everything differently and are less likely to be hurt. If you always train on the track with the stopwatch, you are going to burn out and get discouraged when you don't improve. If the times aren't improving, change the venue and the drills to keep from getting stale.

MENTAL TRAINING

MB: **Earlier you discussed two training pillars: specificity and injury**

TRAINING TALK

prevention. A third pillar you mentioned is the mental side. Can you explain a little about that?

CONNOLLY: Harold's son Jimmy was an NCAA champion in the decathlon and would train with Evelyn from time to time. In 1984, he trained with us at Santa Monica High School, where Harold taught. There was also a parcourse with three heights of bars to jump up and grab. Evelyn had never been able to grab the highest. In a sense it didn't matter if she could touch it since she was still getting the work in, but it was a mind thing. Jimmy told her, "Imagine yourself jumping a little higher than the bar, and see yourself doing that." Evelyn took that little comment from Jimmy, and pop, she was up hanging on that bar screaming in happiness. She just did it. That's the power of the mind.

MB: **Is that something you can develop in your athletes too? How do you go about it?**

CONNOLLY: That brings me to another secret of my coaching. I would never ask an athlete to do something that they were not able to do. Starting right back in the beginning, I only gave them challenges they could accomplish. Success breeds success. I always made the goals realistic. Usually this gains trust. So when I told Evelyn she was ready for a world record, she believed me. It helped her confidence. Without the use of drugs, it took nine years, but it takes time to develop the confidence and achieve the goals.

>> *I would never ask an athlete to do something that they were not able to do.*

It started in the weight room. She was 115 pounds, when I first saw her, and 5'4.5" and had never lifted any kind of weight. At the time, we did a little circuit training in the gym. We put 50 pounds on the universal bench press, and she could barely get it up. I asked myself, "If bench press is not specific to sprinting, why am I having her do this?" Then, I realized it helped women to get aggressive and naturally women aren't as aggressive as men. What helped her get that bar up was squeezing her butt. By letting her use and recruit her strongest muscle, she could pop that bar up. Not long after, I put the weight at 100 pounds. She looked at me like I was crazy, but she did it. Ultimately, she got to a 150-pound free weight bench press. But along the way, we never tried for a PR until she was ready to get it.

TRAINING MEN VERSUS WOMEN

MB: **Technically, you said your approach was different with Evelyn than it would have been with a man. What are some of the main differences you see between male and female athletes?**

CONNOLLY: Women are not physically as strong, and their upper bodies are especially weaker. After that, I think women have a tolerance for more work, and they work harder. I can prove it to you. When I was at UCLA and Jim Bush was coaching the men, my women were working all the time, and the guys were just hanging out.

MB: **The strength difference, then, also impacts technique. How did it affect your approach to coaching technique?**

CONNOLLY: In terms of technique, there were unique things about Evelyn that I had to adapt. Women need to be stronger, and that takes time. One of the things coach Tellez complained about was her technique coming out of the blocks. Women do not have the same strength to hold those positions as men have. It was frustrating because you could practice all you want or say anything you want, but until they get more strength the technique wasn't possible.

I worked with Evelyn for nine years to get to that record in Zurich; we didn't open a magic bottle or find a needle. It was hundredths-of-a-second improvements at a time. If you are not using drugs, it takes longer to develop the strength. As you get stronger the technique improves. It takes

TRAINING TALK

clean women longer to get strong, but they can get there. It is difficult because if you practice starts using bad technique, you might develop bad habits. I was always trying to devise ways to get them into the right positions, while we were also getting stronger. I used a harness; I held them so they could get the right angle; I had them get in their blocks and then, I would push their butt on "go" so they would almost fall. I did everything I could to help that. Maybe guys don't need that since they already have that strength.

6 // ANATOLIY BONDARCHUK

There is one coach whose name has been mentioned in nearly every interview: Dr. Anatoliy Bondarchuk. The reason is simple: he has been the most influential coach on my own coaching, and one of the most influential coaches in the world over the last few decades.

Bondarchuk was, himself, an Olympic champion and world record holder in the hammer throw, and then took over as Soviet national coach for nearly two decades, leading his athletes to over a dozen Olympic medals. His top athlete Yuriy Sedykh won two gold medals and has held the world record for over 30 years. The Soviet team also swept the Olympic podium at the 1976, 1980, 1984, 1988, and 1992 Olympics. They surely would have done the same in 1984 had they not boycotted the Los Angeles games.

Bondarchuk has also had success beyond the hammer. He has coached medalists and world class throwers in the other throwing events. Since moving to Canada in 2005, he helped Dylan Armstrong transition from the hammer throw to shot put and capture bronze at the 2008 Olympics.

The reach of Bondarchuk's influence goes well beyond the world of throwing. In addition to coaching, he is a prolific writer and researcher on train-

TRAINING TALK

ing theory. As Soviet national coach, he had access to data of thousands of athletes, which gave him a perfect opportunity to analyze what was working and experiment with new training concepts. He is best known for popularizing the transfer of training concept and his unique approach to periodization.

Transfer of training is an attempt to quantify and identify which training exercises are the most beneficial for an athlete, using the help of an exercise classification system to do so. Through feedback, coaches can further identify what exercises produces results on the field, but the key is that training should be focused on improving results in your sport. The concept is simple, but often overlooked.

Bondarchuk's approach to periodization builds upon this and is only touched on in passing in this interview. Rather than varying intensity and volume to bring about adaptation, he uses the systematic variation of exercises. He has dozens of different periodization methods built on this premise, but the key is that one or more sets of exercises are used until the athlete fully adapts to them. By repeating the same stimulus, it is easier to adapt. After adaptation, a new stimulus is introduced to continue the process.

I had modeled my training after Bondarchuk's approach before I even met him. As soon as I heard that Bondarchuk was moving to Canada, I was in my car, driving through the mountains and forest to visit him. Over the course of the next decade I got to work with him and learn from him first hand nearly every day. His English was limited to just a few dozen words, but that was somehow enough for him to convey his message. Even as his language improved over the years, his message stayed the same. That is a testament to his method: at its core it just takes some simple ideas and expands upon them.

In this interview, the focus is on the role of maximum strength in training, as well as some related planning and training topics. This interview only grazes the surface of the many ideas Bondarchuk has developed. Learning about his broader approach can also help put this interview in context. A good place to start with that is on the HMMR Media website (www.hmmrmedia.com), which started as a way for me to share my experiences working with him. We often continue to dive into those topics today, including in-depth videos, articles and more on his methods.

LESSONS TO LEARN

- Everybody makes mistakes; it is the ability to learn from them and make a better program the next time that separates the good coaches from the bad. By being able to peak multiple times per year, Bondarchuk's periodization allows him to get more feedback and changes things more quickly, without losing much time on something that does not work.

- Strength does not equal speed. The muscle recruitment in heavy lifting is different than what is required to move an implement at 20 or 30 meters per second. Muscles need to be trained explosively, not slowly.

- Each athlete is different. Coaches always need to ask what is best for *their* athlete. In order to produce the best results the coach needs to find out what works for the athlete, sport, and at that specific time. Some athletes might need more of one ingredient or another, and needs might can change over time. Finding the correct recipe is the coach's principal job.

TRAINING TALK

PLANNING STRATEGIES

MB: **What would you say makes your approach to planning and periodization the most unique?**

BONDARCHUK: I use a different periodization theory. There are 42 methods of periodization I have outlined, but the general idea is that my athletes will reach four, five, or even six peak conditions each year. In the United States, with most methods, athletes have one peak each year. This is first main difference of my approach.

Everybody makes mistakes. If your peak condition takes one year, you are finished. You lost that year. If you make a mistake again then you lose another year. My system is different. For example, I will give my athletes a program with certain intensity, volume, and exercises. After two or three months they will reach peak condition. If the result did not grow, then I made a mistake. Then, I give another system for the second peak condition. If again the results do not grow, I try again. If the first time there is no growth, the second time no growth, but the third time a little growth, then I learned what works.

With six peak conditions each year you have time to learn and make mistakes. Everybody needs different training, and you learn this way what is best. The standard approach is to have a preparation period, competition period, and rest period. We need to change our minds. We do not need to use the whole year for one development period.

MB: **And another central theme is transfer of training. The method and exercises you choose is tightly connected with transfer.**

BONDARCHUK: This is the second difference. There is a big problem in America concerning the development of strength. For 50 years, coaches have been saying maximum strength will increase dynamic speed. It is time to change our minds about this. There are different types of strength. For example, if you do a full squat, your body is moving maximum one or two meters per second. If you shot put, your body moves up to 16 meters per second for an elite result. In the hammer throw, the implement is moving at 32 meters per second. Do not always think about maximum strength; think about explosive muscles. It's about maximum speed not maximum strength. If you change your mind, you will start using different methods.

THE ROLE OF MAXIMUM STRENGTH AND MUSCLE FIBER

MB: **Yuriy Sedykh was one of your top athletes. He was a two-time Olympic champion, yet never had the maximum strength numbers of his competitors, correct?**

BONDARCHUK: Yuriy did not have the huge muscles of the other athletes, but he threw far because he used a different system. We trained together 20 years, and, during this time, he did not use full squats. He would only sometimes use half squats, but not with 250 or 300 kilograms, but doing 180 kilograms fast.

I also like to talk about my friend. Back in 1962, he had a bench press result of 320 kilograms. In the full squat, he did 350 kilograms, but he only threw 17.20 meters in the shot put. Christian Cantwell, for example, has

TRAINING TALK

around a 305-kilogram bench and over 22 meters in the shot put. And Al Feuerbach could only bench about 165 kilograms but set the world record at 21.81 meters in 1973, but he had fantastic explosive muscles.

MB: **Are you referring to fast-twitch muscles when you are talking about "explosive" muscles?**

BONDARCHUK: You need to think about athletes with explosive muscles. Athletes have two kinds of muscle fiber: slow and fast types. If athletes have 70% slow and 30%, fast they will not get a good result. You need to find athletes with 70% or more explosive muscles.

In my book on throwing, I have some statistics about what levels of strength are needed. If you look at the men's discus throwers around 65 meters we saw the worst athletes around 125 kilograms in the snatch and the best athletes at 165 kilograms. If worst result is 125 kilograms and this is enough for 65 or 70 meters, then you do not need 165 kilograms. In the hammer, Yuriy Sedykh had a snatch of 120 kilograms. Tibor Gecsek had 160 kilograms. The same was the case in the clean; Yuriy had 165 kilograms and Gecsek had 205 kilograms. Even I had a result of 190 kilograms, but I only threw 77.42 meters and Yuriy threw 86.74 meters. He did not have big results in snatch and clean, but he had explosive muscle.

MB: **The type of muscle we have is mostly predetermined, but we can still develop it to get the most out of what we have. How do you go about developing these explosive muscles?**

BONDARCHUK: In training, you need to use the explosive muscle. If you are looking for maximum strength in the snatch and you can only do 100 kilograms, then use 40, 50 or 60 kilograms to develop speed in training. This is a different idea. Think about speed, speed, speed; fast, fast, fast.

There are lots of methods, though, to develop all types of strength. You must choose for your athletes. Some athletes need 90-95% intensities to develop maximum strength. Others need 80-85%. Somebody uses 80% and results grow. Others use it, and their results go down. Everybody is different; different muscle, different everything. You must know this general idea, and after the general idea, you must transfer to your athlete. This is true for all parts of training, e.g. with heavy implements in the hammer throw, somebody needs an 8-kilogram hammer, somebody a 12-kilogram. Everybody must first use the scientific general idea and then individualize it.

No scientist or coach can tell you what to do. Everyone is different, and what works also changes. If you find a system that works for a 16-meter shot putter, it must change to keep working as the body grows. If an athlete throws 16 meters, you can do 50-60 tons per month. With 18 meters you might need 100 tons. You need to think about long-term training and each peak condition needs to be a better system.

> >> No scientist or coach can tell you what to do. Everyone is different, and what works also changes.

TRAINING FAST

MB: If you are lifting a lot at submaximal intensities, is it faster just because of less weight or do the athletes also attempt to move it as fast as possible?

BONDARCHUK: You always ask the question to yourself: what do I need for my athlete. If you want speed, you must move it fast. Some people say for development of maximum strength you need 90% intensity. But 60% can also develop maximum strength. For example, many reps at 60% can have same effect as one rep at 90%, but you also develop speed-strength with the lower weight. If you just use 90%, you do not develop speed. If an athlete needs speed, they need to use this zone. If the intensity is down, you can move faster. But you also have to pay attention, since more repetitions can cause exhaustion. If your athlete is exhausted, that will not promote speed.

TRAINING TALK

MB: **Often we use sets with five reps. Is there anything special about this?**

BONDARCHUK: There is not a big difference between five and six reps; the results are the same. There is just a big difference between one or two reps and 15 reps, but, between five and six there is not much difference. Again, you need to see what is best for your athlete.

MB: **Is this approach just for the throws, or for all speed sports? For example, in baseball or boxing, you need speed, and the implements weigh less or weigh nothing. Would your approach change there?**

BONDARCHUK: Every kind of sport is different, and you need to think about the specific needs. Baseball needs a lot of explosive muscles. Even within throwing events, there are differences. Let's say that your tonnage for a hammer thrower is broken up into 50% for maximum strength development and 50% for maximum speed. In the javelin, it might be 30% for maximum strength and 70% for maximum speed. Every sport is a little different. The question is always: what do I need for my athlete?

But it is not 100% maximum strength. This is big problem in the United States. This is a problem in the head. Everyone thinks they need maximum strength for the past 50 years. They think that with maximum strength comes maximum speed. This is an old idea. Forget about it; it's a mistake. Some sports like track and field need maximum speed. Without maximum speed you cannot have a maximum result. Maximum strength is a tractor. Maximum speed is a Ferrari. This is a different car, a different idea.

MB: **People often think you are trying to say that maximum strength is not important, but that isn't the case at all. You are just saying that you only need so much of it, correct?**

BONDARCHUK: It is not that you need one or the other. You need everything. You just have to decide what level of each you need. What is enough? We talked about this before, e.g. with Feuerbach he had just 165

> **>> Maximum strength is a tractor. Maximum impact is a Ferrari. This is a different car, a different idea.**

kilograms in the bench, but Cantwell has over 300 kilograms and both threw around 22 meters. Maybe 165 is enough for 22 meters, and 300 is definitely more than enough.

MB: **Obviously, this is not the only approach to training. People have thrown far with other systems too. What makes this system better?**

BONDARCHUK: One more thing. I told you about my system, but there are lots of good systems. Other systems like the German or US system have good results. I think my system is not bad, but others work too. Try it. If the system does not produce results try something else. Every coach makes mistakes. A coach just needs to admit when he is wrong and study all the time to find the right answer. I change my system every five years.

I have athletes come to me and want to try some new exercise or method. I have no problem trying another system. Dylan could already bench press over 200 kilograms when I started coaching him, but he kept talking about how Cantwell can bench press over 300 kilograms. I told him it didn't have transfer, but he kept asking. So we said we would try one program with more volume and intensity. He thought if he could increase it, then he could throw further. After two months, he had a bench press of 240 kilograms already. His best result in the shot put the previous season was 21.40 meters, but his training results went down to 19.65 meters. So I asked Dylan, "Does it have transfer or not?" That is the question for all coaches.

7 // DEREK EVELY

No doubt that Bondarchuk has some thought-provoking ideas, but a common criticism is that he focuses more on the theory than the practice. He, no doubt, has the practical experience that gives gravitas to what he says, but he is hesitant to tell others how to train for the simple reason that everyone is different. His training theory is built around the premise that training needs to be tailored to an individual and their event; to hand out a training plan template would be contrary to his underlying beliefs.

To learn the practical side of Bondarchuk's methods, you need to see him work and try things for yourself. I've had the chance to learn hands-on from Bondarchuk, and that definitely gives me an advantage in applying his theories to practice. Another coach that has done this is Derek Evely. He not only got to coach alongside Bondarchuk for a year, but he has since had more than a decade of experience putting it into practice with his athletes.

Evely started his career in Canada at the Kamloops Track Club. As a coach, Evely trained Shane Niemi to a national junior record of 45.83 seconds in the 400 meters. He guided a young Gary Reed, who went on to win a silver medal in the 800 meters at the 2007 World Championships. He also led Dylan Armstrong to a North American junior record and silver medal at the World Junior Championships in the hammer throw. It was

TRAINING TALK

Armstrong that brought Evely together with Bondarchuk. Armstrong was transitioning to the shot put and approaching 20 meters, and Evely hired Bondarchuk to move to Canada to help with the project.

While Bondarchuk has stayed in Kamloops ever since, Evely has moved around the world. After a season working alongside Bondarchuk, he left to head the Canadian Athletics Coaching Centre in Edmonton. There, he helped develop a leading online coaching resource and guide a long-sprint group that included world 400-meter medalist Tyler Christopher and Canadian national 400-meter hurdle record holder Adam Kunkel.

From 2009 to 2012, Evely worked as director of the Loughborough University High Performance Centre, one of the UK's two national training centers in the lead up to their home 2012 Olympics. There he also guided Sophie Hitchon to a World Junior Championships hammer throw title. In the Olympic qualifying round she also threw a British record to make the Olympic final at age 21. After the Olympics, he has returned to Kamloops where he continues to consult, coach, and share his ideas on the new website www.EveltrakSport.com.

Evely's experience coaching in different environments, working with different events, and learning from coaches around the world has given him a big advantage in understanding how and where Bondarchuk's concepts can fit in.

In our interview, we discussed how he applies the methods, how they can be adapted to a variety of events, and, most importantly, a closer look at how he decides to adapt exercises and training to make them better for his athletes. The discussion on this final point is often very hammer throw-specific, but the process is the most interesting since it requires you to focus on finding out what your athlete needs. The core of the conversation took place in 2011 as he was preparing Hitchon for the Olympics, although a few responses from our chat in 2013 have also been integrated to dive deeper into some of the topics discussed.

LESSONS TO LEARN

- Exercise selection should not be done lightly. As a coach you will never pick the perfect exercises to use, but you can make educated guesses based on the background of the athlete and the dynamics of the sport you are training for. More important is the data you collect after you use a set of exercises. From this data you can tell what works and better tailor future training.

- A drill is an exercise, so you need to make sure that it transfers just as you would with any other exercise. Sometimes, drills stray so far from the competitive movement that they no longer help. Again, keep in mind the demands of the event, and ensure they are in any drills you use, so that technical gains in the drill will transfer to the sport.

- Bondarchuk's methods can be easily adapted for other events. People think of Bondarchuk as a hammer coach, and he is; but Evely provides examples below of how he has implemented the concepts in training sprinters, jumpers, and more.

TRAINING TALK

FINDING AND CREATING THE RIGHT EXERCISES

MB: One of the more difficult things for you to learn watching Bondarchuk is how he chooses exercises for his athletes. The big picture is easy: more throwing and special strength exercises, no exercises like curls and the bench press which are not specific to the hammer. At the detailed level, why does he pick a 6.3-kilogram hammer to throw instead of a 6-kilogram hammer or the back squat instead of the front squat?

We've both said his process feels almost random at times. I am sure there is some methodology to how he chooses them. What is your approach to exercise selection in those types of situations?

EVELY: I actually asked Dr. B one day while we were sitting there, "How do you choose which exercises you use?" He basically said that if he does not know the athlete well enough and does not have an idea of what will work well with that athlete, then he just experiments. He tries different things at random. Of course, these are educated guesses, but he throws everything against the wall to see what sticks. So, that is how it starts.

Then after that, over time and over the years of changing the programs and the variations he applies, he will remember what works and what doesn't. The odd thing about that is that he rarely, if ever, goes back and presents the exact same training program to an athlete. The combination of exercises are almost always different, but he almost always has an idea of what exercises work and what do not with particular athletes.

MB: How then do you go about determining what exercises work with your athletes? For example now you are working with Sophie Hitchon and Mark Dry in the hammer throw. What does this process look like with their training?

EVELY: When I left Kamloops in 2005 I spent five or five years in Edmonton, where I only coached the sprints and applied a lot of this methodology. Since 2009, I've been applying this to the hammer, and it is really interesting for me. As I start to sort a lot of this stuff out, I'm starting to see a lot of the stuff I read come to life. Here is a really good example: look at the women's hammer throw correlations in Dr. Bondarchuk's transfer of training book for various non-specific exercises, those that would fall into the SPE (special preparation exercises) category, such as the Olympic lifts, squats, things like that. With many of the exercises there is more transfer around the 55-, 60-, 65-meter mark than there is over 70 meters. Now that has been exactly my experience.

I keep very detailed records of our training and how far we throw every day. I went back for both Mark and Sophie for last season, and that gave me a chart with a curve of the throwing distances over the entire year. I took this chart and overlaid the volumes that we did with every other type of training that was in the program at various times. So, for instance, I would overlay the volume of special throws, general strength and maximal strength. When I looked at the maximal strength I actually found that when we were doing Olympic lifts in particular, we usually got a pretty good bounce off of that. To me that meant there was obviously some transfer, not a huge amount of transfer, but it was enough of an effect that I couldn't ignore it.

Now, when we look at it this year, there is not as much. But of course now Sophie has gone from being a 60- to 65-meter thrower to a 65- to 70-meter thrower. She has gone up a class. So to me, it is interesting that now I'm seeing exactly what the book and Dr. Bondarchuk's research says. There is still a little bit of transfer, so I make sure it is always in the program, but I'm not seeing as much as I did last year.

MB: **In one of your presentations, you discussed that you choose and execute exercises for the hammer throw with two things in mind. First, the hammer throw is the only track and field event where the athlete keeps contact with the ground at all times, and the goal is to lengthen the amount of ground contact. Second, hammer throwers must work together with an external object. These points make the hammer throw**

TRAINING TALK

unique. As a result, you have adapted how you do plyometrics with your throwers. Can you explain a little about your thought process in selecting what jumps to use? I think this thought process could be applied to other sports and events, if you identify their individual needs of each event.

EVELY: I think leaving the ground quickly is contrary to all the throws, but this is true especially for the hammer. I think a lot of coaches get lured and attached to hurdle hops and other traditional jump exercises, which are a great way to develop explosive strength, but when you look at the physical parameters of the exercise, it is not terribly specific to the hammer throw. In the hammer you are applying force through the double support phase for as long as you can. The time in which the athlete applies force to the implement is massive compared to any other event, especially when compared to non-throwing events. And the athlete has to apply force while under an incredible load, so that makes it unique as well. I simply think that these unique characteristics need to be taken into account when selecting exercises for the development of form, especially when we are looking for specific development exercises.

The problem with hurdle hops and other traditional jump exercises is that not only are they not specific enough, but they carry with them a big risk of injury. They are tempting to employ and many athletes, especially talented ones, like to do them because in this area, they can rival if not exceed their sprinters and jumpers. Let's face it, anytime a thrower can out-perform a sprinter or jumper in public, it is a very good thing. But, even then, you have to ask yourself what you are trying to accomplish.

MB: **So if you are not using hurdle hops, what jumping exercises are you using?**

EVELY: For me, intense exercise selection must follow the principle of polarization of intensity. Exercises need to be either specific and intense enough to highly transfer, or they need to be non-specific enough to contribute simply to general athletic abilities and recovery processes. Anything in the middle has to be employed with great caution, otherwise they will exploit precious energy reserves (reserves better spent on throwing, in my opinion) yet not contribute greatly to any specific progress in form development. I see hurdle hops and other general jumps routines as perfect anti-examples of this.

>> Intense exercise selection must follow the principle of polarization of intensity.

Now, having said all this, there is a place for jumps in the program, but if you are trying to create a jumping exercise that is an specific developmental exercise you have to think about the transfer. Ask yourself, "What are the kinetic parameters of the hammer throw?" and design and prescribe accordingly.

We answered that by using jumping exercises that were more specific. For example, jumping onto a 50- or 60-centimeter box with dumbbells in your hands and then jumping off the box, but landing seated on a high jump mat. This lengthens the amortization and extension phases so that (a) the kinetics are more similar to the demands of the hammer event, (b) you are not hitting the ground hard, and (c) it is under load. I found that to be far more effective and much healthier.

MB: **How about sprinting exercises? Like jumps, those are used to develop explosive strength and put an emphasis on minimizing ground contact times.**

EVELY: We use sprints occasionally. It is an exercise like anything else, so why not consider it? I do not look at sprinting with the idea of creating a specific transfer. I see the speed work clearly as a more general exercise. It is using similar muscles, but stimulating somewhat different systems. And that's why we do not go beyond 20 or 30 meters. We are trying to work

TRAINING TALK

on push development off the ground and turnover, but it is also kind of a recovery exercise for them that develops some general speed qualities, which I think are important. We don't do anything close to the volumes an actual sprinter would, simply to respect the polarization principle I mentioned above.

MB: **What is a sprint protocol like for one of your throwers?**

EVELY: The speed sessions are comprised mostly of 10- to 30-meter runs, but we will draw it out to 40- or 50-meters as the development cycle moves forward. They will do no more than 150 meters total in a session. I keep it in there because both athletes I coach are quite athletic and like to do it, and I believe it helps their basic speed and athleticism. We only use it in the first two or three cycles of the year and then I remove it as we get closer to the competitive season, just because I don't want that type of work to start to draw away from actual throwing. When we do include it, I keep it very limited. We'll do one sprint and one tempo running session a week.

The problem with this kind of work is when you start to do stupid things with it. You are not going to take a thrower and give them a speed endurance workout because you're talking about a week's recovery. You know what I mean? There is no real point going out beyond 50- or 60-meters because (a) you're going to risk injury and (b) you're probably going to tap into the nervous or lactate systems a bit too much and you're going to kill their throwing for the next two to three days, if not longer. So those are some of the things I keep in mind when I prescribe speed.

In terms of tempo running, it is very innocuous in its prescription, such as eight to 10 x 100 meters on the grass. Nothing is timed. They can go as slow as they want and it basically just gives them 10-15 minutes of basic aerobic work at the end of the week.

MB: **Dr. Bondarchuk told me he doesn't include sprinting in the workouts for hammer throwers to develop speed because he feels there is a** big difference between rotational speed and linear speed. Also I think another factor is that the hammer, an external factor, also helps generate the speed rather than just the body alone.

EVELY: I agree. Sophie was a former youth sprinter. She is good at it, likes it, and it gives her confidence. We were at a national training center, and she was as fast as the best sprinters there over 20 or 30 meters. We used it mainly in the developmental cycles that correspond with fall and winter because it provided a nice change of stimulus.

Remember, a very big concept in this system can be summed up in the old adage, "A change is as good as a rest." It worked for her and Mark (to a lesser degree), but I was always clear with myself why I was doing it. I was not giving them sprints because I was expecting a direct transfer. I was giving them sprints to develop some general speed qualities; otherwise it was just another exercise like cleans or back extensions.

MAXIMUM STRENGTH & INCORPORATING OTHER METHODS

MB: **You said most of your stuff is based on Bondarchuk, but obviously you are incorporating some other stuff. What are some of the other things you are trying to incorporate, and how do you fit those into his methods?**

EVELY: For my throwers I run a very similar program structurally. The only reason I say it is not exactly the same as Dr. B's is because I don't fully understand the ins and outs of how Dr. B implements everything he does within his own program. It would be presumptuous for me to say that I copy it, and I would never copy it anyways. If I wasn't really able to figure something out, I do my own thing with what makes sense to me.

For me the big objective is trying to determine the number of sessions it takes for an athlete to reach peak form. That's the first question. The second question is what group of exercises and what weights of implements will give us the best reaction? And the third question is then how do I periodize that? You can't just simply keep reintroducing cycles.

TRAINING TALK

That was the big question that I had after 2010 so I sat down with Dr. B and he explained it to me: there needs to be a rest cycle. What does that mean? I realized that rest could also mean "realization," so I have gone with that in some cases, but it is still the trickiest part for me, what to do between cycles. We've been playing around with a few things regarding rest and realization approaches. To me, this is as individual as the development period. So that's where it's been a little bit tricky.

One area that is a little different for me, in comparison to Dr. B, is that I do employ a little more maximal strength than Dr. B does. However, I don't believe in implementing it to the point where it affects the reaction. That's the key to it. I say that because most of the guys I work with here are not Dylan. When I turned Dylan over to Dr. B, he didn't need any more maximal strength. He was about the strongest guy on the planet back then, and he's probably been riding that wave for a while. But these guys I work with now need a little bit more of it.

Another aspect of our program, which in some ways is very similar to what Dr. B does, is to implement some kind of post-throwing strength routine that covers all of the different bases in terms of movement experience. I've drawn heavily from Dan Pfaff in that area in that I use ancillary strength circuits and the structure he uses in his programs. I've been using those for about 15 years now, and they've evolved and adapted nicely from his program. That is one key idea I got from Dan: performance and health can be created and maintained through proper exercise prescription. I think that's a really key area that we do really well. I try to set those up so that they cover all of the different movement planes: sagittal, frontal, and transverse planes when prescribing movements/exercises. There's a lot of twisting, a lot of side bending, and of course, a healthy dose of sagittal because almost everything's sagittal. I try to keep it pretty balanced.

I also include various jumping exercises, but I keep the volume pretty low. We don't do any more than 8-12 repetitions of jumps in a single session. But with the hammer guys, they are all loaded jumps. We do them all with dumbbells in the hands. With the hammer guys, I do absolutely nothing that is reaction off the ground, as I described earlier.

MB: **Regarding maximum strength, I kind of had the same impression, just looking at how different athletes have done well under Bondarchuk or kind of struggled. It seems that those that come in with a lot more maximum strength in the first place, like Dylan, that type of program is not a problem. But there are definitely some athletes that come in on the weaker side, and if they don't get up to that certain minimum level of strength, his program doesn't help to bring you up to it very well. I mean, over time it works, as was the case with Justin Rodhe who came in relatively weak and got quite strong with Bondarchuk's slow and steady approach.**

EVELY: That's a sore spot with some strength and conditioning types who believe that the only way to get strong is through spending gross amounts of energy in the gym. I don't have a definitive answer on that one, but I have noticed that throwing the hammer a lot will increase your cleans, I am sure of this. This is the same as how doing sprints will increase your step ups or squats. I can't say that the opposite is true with quite as much confidence, although I do believe these are worthwhile pursuits if implemented with a rational and systematic methodology.

MB: **My own strength levels were not that high coming in, but after years of working with him, I was fooling around in the weight room this winter and doing cleans and I'm much stronger than I was five years ago and I haven't lifted more than 70% in that time. It works over the long term, but you're not going to get the quick gains with the system.**

EVELY: I think that the single most difficult hurdle in describing Dr. B's methodology is interpretation. I've done a number of presentations both with Dr. Bondarchuk and without him, and I've talked to a lot of throws coaches about this because they hear the stories. They hear it about Dylan most of all, how he doesn't really lift heavy; he doesn't lift anything over a

TRAINING TALK

certain amount of weight. It really messes with a lot of people's heads, and they really battle with that kind of concept, and I see why, but the biggest problem with it is that people look at it in such black and white terms, and they struggle with getting what the real message is.

The real message is not that you don't do maximal strength, or even that maximal strength doesn't transfer. The real message is: how much do you need and once you're there then what are you going to do? People think that Bondarchuk's message is, "Don't do any maximal strength." That is not it at all. You absolutely need a certain level of it, and you need a fairly high level relative to most athletes. Let's face it; you're not going to throw 20 meters in the shot with only a 100-kilogram bench. Maybe someone's done it, but it is going to be the exception not the rule. So, absolutely you need it. The problem is we love the weight room, especially in North America. At the point where the pursuit of absolute strength starts taking away from the throwing, then you have to ask yourself is this all worth it or is there something else I could be doing or implementing that may pay bigger dividends.

In order to get very strong in a short period of time, you have to lift a lot and it will really affect your throwing. If this is your plan, then fine, but block periodization schemes are difficult to implement and can wreak havoc on event-specific abilities. You have to look at it over the long term.

To me it has always been that the biggest struggle is getting that concept through to people. They see it one way or the other; no balance or rational implementation. And it's unfortunate, but I guess it is the black and white recipe mentality that is out there with a lot of people. You have to make judgments for each and every single athlete you coach. And their programs are all going to look different or be implemented differently, based upon their needs. It is a simple concept, really.

MB: **You mentioned Dylan's strength levels before he started working with Bondarchuk, but even there you had a long-term approach, correct?**

Evely

EVELY: Dylan was incredibly strong. And although we did more heavy lifting than he does now, I was actually really cautious with him through the years that we didn't go too heavy with him because there was such a potential for abuse. I always kept him within four to six reps range. We pretty much stuck to 65-80% loads, sometimes 85% and moved things as fast as possible, but when he was using 85% loads, he was using a lot of weight simply because he was so strong out of the gate. Other than bench, we rarely went into the one to three rep range or max intensities.

He loved doing it, and he loved getting strong, and he really thought that was his forte; but he was way stronger than anybody needs to be to throw far. It certainly didn't hurt him when Dr. B came along and started in another direction. He was ready for it. Where we went wrong was the emphasis on the strength program. Even though we didn't lift as much as many other programs, if I had to do it all over again, I would have had him throw more and lift less.

Dylan actually struggled that first year with Dr. B. He threw 19.83 prior to Dr. B's arrival and was progressing quite well. Then Dr. B came and he threw 20.62, but he didn't throw farther than 19.83 in another meet that whole year, if I remember right. I think this relative lack of improvement was in part due to his own mental struggles with the change in programs. Before the 20.62 meters, he struggled with the concept of not lifting as heavy as we were. I remember in the first few months under Dr. B, I just kept saying to him, "Just put your head down, don't ask questions, and do what he says." Then, of course, he eventually came around to Dr. B's ways. He has never looked back and that has made all the difference in the world. Now that he has bought into it 100%, it works. And of course now we have seen the pattern with Kibwé Johnson.

So my point here is that he had such a huge reserve of strength when Dr. B came, he was able to make the shift quite easily in a physical sense because in fact it was exactly what he needed: more throwing/special exercises and less lifting. But that may not be the same for everyone in such a dramatic

TRAINING TALK

fashion. As you say, the program Dr. B employs still develops maximal strength, it just does it in a different fashion and across a longer period. And I believe this approach to be more rational. Even a coach who is presented with a weak athlete needs to consider this approach and adapt as needed; it is not the ins and outs that one needs to consider but the philosophy that underpins the program.

THE OFFSEASON

MB: **You mentioned earlier a little about rest periods during the year. I'd like your thoughts on the off season. With Dr. Bondarchuk, the off season is non-existent or very, very short. We just train throughout the year. Are you doing the same? Just taking a few weeks off?**

EVELY: Yes. I learned that the hard way with Sophie last year. After World Juniors, she took three weeks off. It was probably a mistake because when she came back, it took her a full period of training to get back to what you would call a reasonable shape. She just struggled getting back into it. So I think probably this next year, we'll do nothing more than a week, two tops. She cannot afford to take that much time off. I don't regret doing it because she needed the mental rest, but physically it was tough.

MB: **Every once in a while I'll read an interview with a college or pro thrower that says they got tired after the season and took a few months off. Every time, I think, "This is going to be a tough year" and most of the time it turns out that way.**

EVELY: I learned that with sprinters, again, the hard way. This is not a foreign concept to me because with sprinters it is very much like that. This is what a lot of coaches don't realize. When you get an athlete and they are in peak form, or over a number of years they've risen to a high level, if you lose that either through injury or forced time off, it is very difficult to get back to where you were; very difficult. Once they're up there, you really don't want to let them get away from it for too long. Sure, different program designs may call for variances in the amount of specific work and intensities, but we are talking here about allowing the system to get away from specific work completely or near completely for weeks or months on end.

This is why traditional stage methodologies are not ideal, especially for speed-power events; why go back each year at the beginning and train as if you are out of shape when two or three weeks before that you were in the shape of your life? I'm sure in some cases long rest periods are necessary, but for me I would just really try not to let an athlete get into that situation in the first place. It's a very long, slow process over years that gets an athlete to a really high level of specific fitness so to purposefully direct them away from that state makes no sense to me. And, the more talented they are, the more this is true. To get them to a really high level, once they are there, you cannot let them get too far away from it. Otherwise, it just takes too long to get it back. In some cases, they don't come back.

BONDARCHUK FOR NON-THROWERS

MB: **When you were coaching the sprints, were you still following Bondarchuk's methods?**

EVELY: Well, to begin with, the way Kevin Tyler and I were already setting up our sprint periodization and methodology is very similar to how a sprint program would work under Bondarchuk's methodology. I just sort of formalized it in terms of looking at the athlete's reaction and particularly the number of sessions it would take for an athlete to reach peak form. That is one of the key elements of his whole methodology: that you understand what amount of specific training or more specifically exposures to specific training it takes for an athlete to reach peak condition. We found that with a lot of our sprinters, they were coming into form after about 36-45 sessions with a mixture of various types of speed training, and that is what we were doing already.

Knowing this number or range is incredibly helpful when designing a program because it gives you a base from which to plan, rather than simply following traditional formats (i.e., sprint three times per week, start in

TRAINING TALK

September, run indoors, etc.). Once you know this, you can get creative and customize the periodization; if you know your athlete peaks around 40 sessions, this may be where you will want to compete, simply count back and set the periodization up that way.

If you look at the first period of a normal double or triple periodization sprint program that starts in say late September or early October, it gives a good example of what we are discussing. Speed is typically built up to maybe three speed sessions a week of acceleration, max speed, or some form of speed/special/specific endurance and then tapers off into an indoor season. It usually takes most athletes about 12-15 weeks to come into form and they're ready to race. Some are different, but generally, this has been our experience. If you take 12-15 weeks and multiply it by three speed sessions a week, what do you get? You get about 36-45. That's what we were doing in the past, but once we realized this, it made planning even more precise.

I also started to count those numbers for various athletes by analyzing performances and then began to look at other successful sprint programs and saw similar numbers there too. So it was very interesting to me because generally speaking, these are similar numbers to many athletes in throws. So, it wasn't so much that we made a conscious attempt at applying his methods, it was more that we were merely formalizing our own approach by thinking about it the way Dr. Bondarchuk thinks about it.

MB: **How were you measuring the reaction to the program in the sprints? With the throws it is easy and precise because you simply measure the distance thrown in training mark, but in the sprints it seems like it would be more difficult.**

EVELY: Yeah, at times it is. I probably wasn't as detailed and accurate as I am in the throws. It is a bit easier in the throws, there is no question, but it can be done in the sprints fairly easily: just record times over training distances.

MB: **Would a workout be replicated the same way as with Bondarchuk? Most of the time with Bondarchuk, we have one workout we'll do 10 times a week or two programs that we alternate during the week. For example, we'd throw the same weight hammer at each session. Was it the same in the sprints, or is there more variety so that you aren't doing the same 50-meter sprints every morning and afternoon?**

EVELY: In the sprints, you can't do five or 10 speed sessions as week. You can't really do more than three speed workouts a week, maybe four if you have great weather and superior therapists working with you. And don't forget that in our case, we were in Edmonton training indoors on an old track, so most of the time it was more like two sessions. I suspect if you were training on a good training track in the southern US or Europe you could probably get away with more like three to four sessions a week.

That also has implications on how you would periodize your program. If you're in Canada and doing just two sessions a week compared to in the southern US and doing four with a really good cracker jack therapy team behind you, that will double the number of peak forms that you will be able to have during a year, which is huge.

As for variation in the distances, this is pretty important. Correct, you can't run the same distances in each workout. You must, to some degree, cover the bases in terms of developing the required speed abilities within each cycle, so this gets a little tricky, but I do not think such variance will delay or confuse the adaptation, as long as you stay within the specific demands the event requires. The big question is: how does one force adaptation in the following periods and still stay within these specific demands? In other words, how does one provide a change in stimulus (different distances) while at the same time keeping the work specific? It is tough because the window of specificity in terms of the specific demands for the sprints is relatively small. This is why complex methodologies that employ year-round speed work are much harder to employ, but pay bigger dividends.

TRAINING TALK

MB: **It also seems like also in the javelin they cannot replicate the throwing density that Bondarchuk applies in the shot put and hammer. The intensity is higher and so is the impact on the body. I think it might be a similar approach there.**

EVELY: Absolutely, it is very much the same, but it depends on how you look at it. If you are talking about throwing the javelin, then it probably can only be done two, maybe a maximum three, times a week. We have Esa Utriainen here at our center in Loughborough; he's our national event coach in the javelin, and I see his guys train every day. Now they throw every day, but they are throwing balls, javelins, and different things. If you look at it that way, they are throwing the javelin pretty much every day, they just aren't throwing the actual javelin. It all depends on how you look at it.

MB: **You see that when he's training Deana Zelinka in the javelin. She probably won't touch a real javelin that much, especially during the winter season since they are indoors and she can't throw a real javelin. So she just throws a lot of balls. She's getting the same movement in. It's not the exact competitive exercise, but it's pretty close.**

EVELY: In some events, the theories seem difficult to apply, but you can still transfer the same concepts. Can you high jump five to eight times a week? No. It's impossible. But, you can do some kind of jumps, some kind of lower amplitude jumping almost every day, and I've seen guys do that. Even then you need to be extremely careful. It all depends on how you interpret what you see and hear from this type of methodology. Like with anything, but especially with this, you have to interpret it with a dose of common sense.

MB: **Exactly. That's very important. If you just think about it strictly from the reading, you would just apply the same program to the javelin, but you realize that it wouldn't work and that there are other ways to do it. You have to bring the common sense in.**

EVELY: I think the trickiest thing to do is figure out how to measure reaction. It is easy in the hammer when you can throw and measure every day. If you are throwing a ball against a wall as a javelin thrower, how are you going to know? The problem is where you are using this methodology, and you can't measure or can only get limited data. I think you just do it and use whatever data you can get. I think it still works. It's trickier, involves some extrapolation, but it still works.

DRILLS

MB: **Getting back to transfer and understanding the demands of your sport, you mentioned that the hammer throw is unique because throwers have to negotiate the force of an external object. Why is this so important and how does it impact your training?**

EVELY: From what I can tell, there are only two events in athletics where you are using an implement, and the implement puts a significant amount of force back on the athlete. One is the pole vault, where energy is transferred into the pole, and then released back into the athlete when the pole is straightened. The other is the hammer, where the ever-increasing pull of the ball has to be increasingly negotiated by the athlete. The athlete is impacted by that, and this presents a unique environment.

With the hammer, it is very important that coaches understand this. Think about drills: if you are doing a drill that slows the event down to the point where the pull of the hammer is gone, it creates a completely different effect. I have never thrown the hammer, and even I can tell you that. I question the amount of non-specific drills coaches use that do not create that force. It is not that you shouldn't do these drills, but you really need to understand why you are doing them.

The same goes with certain specific strength exercises. Just because they are in a certain position that resembles positions you see in a frame-by-frame analysis, it does not necessarily make that exercise specific. One needs to take into consideration the forces present during a throw. Some-

TRAINING TALK

times we are teaching the exact opposite of what the athlete will feel when they are throwing the hammer. The solution we came up with, which everyone is familiar with, is to use heavier hammers. If you want to do a drill and slow everything down, the solution I found was to use a heavy hammer with some type of turning activity.

MB: **What is an example of how you might use the heavy hammer in place of a drill or as a drill?**

EVELY: After throwing we employed heavy hammer turns. We would start with an entry followed by four turns in a circle just to slow things down, and it also taught you to negotiate the force in a big way. With both Sophie Hitchon and Mark Dry, these exercises were incredibly important and had a big influence on their hammer strength and technique. I found that regardless of the time of year or development cycle we were in, we needed to be doing some form of this exercise. Sophie would use up to a 9-kilogram hammer and Mark up to 20-kilograms. Other than that, I just don't see where you can do a lot of other drills, unless they are one or two turn throws, where you actually have to negotiate that force. A lot of people forget that.

It is a lot different when you have to deal with an implement that is putting force back into you. Without that force you cannot reach the same positions and even if you do, they are never truly the same. It may look the same, but it is different without the pull of the ball.

A similar example is running drills. A lot of people do running drills to improve their running technique, but there is no correlation between people that do good running drills and have good sprinting technique. Now, there is a place for running drills if you are trying to teach a specific concept to the athlete or trying to re-educate faulty patterns, and my elite sprint coaching friends are very good at this. But I don't do a lot of them with sprinters in an effort to teach technique. I do two or three drills designed to teach force application, but other than that, we just run and we make corrections when we are running like my throwers do when we are throwing.

MB: **Do you think it might be different in the shot put, where not as many outside forces are acting on the athlete?**

EVELY: I don't think it applies as much there. If you do a glide into a power position, this is not that much different with or without the shot put in the hand, for an experienced thrower. You can do drills and they are more effective in the shot put. But even then the timing is a little different than the full throw. Drills are good tools when you have a big problem or are working with a beginner, but if things are going well then I prefer to just throw.

> >> *It's all pretty straightforward and simple. Look closely at the event mechanics and force application requirements and what you are trying to achieve.*

In summary, it's all pretty straightforward and simple. Look closely at the event mechanics and force application requirements and what you are trying to achieve. Some of these points, in my experience, are things that people don't often think about, especially whether each exercise transfers. We just do these exercises, such as jumps or drills, because we think any explosive exercise will transfer, but we don't take a hard look at what we are doing. It doesn't make any sense.

PART II //
ON THE FIELD

Track and field coaches have it easy. Our athletes have one movement to execute and one way to measure it. For example, my athletes simply have to throw the hammer and a tape measure gives me an immediate objective evaluation of whether we're doing it well. In other sports, things are not so straightforward.

Field, court, and team sports involve a complex combination of movements, and success is more difficult to measure. With so many movements, it becomes more difficult to identify the transfer of training. Will an improvement in a training exercise help improve performance on the field? To answer this question you have to first look at what movements the exercise might improve.

Next, you have to look at how important each of those movements is in the overall context of the game. To make things more complicated, you also need to determine a way to evaluate the player's improvement in order to measure the amount of transfer. A string of wins after implementing a new exercise could be due to transfer of training, but it also could, just as easily, be the result of weak competition or improved tactics.

These are just some of the challenging issues confronting strength and conditioning coaches in field sports. In this part, we talk with leading practitioners in various field sports: coach and theorist Frans Bosch, international rubgy coaches John Pryor and John Kiely, soccer coach Dave Tenney, and NFL coach Tom Myslinski. They represent three sports, and even more backgrounds and philosophies.

TRAINING TALK

The first two talks are with Dave Tenney and Tom Myslinski. Tenney explains how he focuses on the on-field work, as that is soccer's version of specific strength. He uses technology to identify the elements lacking in on-field training so that he can create a solid supplemental off-field program. Tom Myslinksi has a specific approach to defining the needs of each of the 22 players on the field and stabilizing the loads off the field to get a better grasp of which elements are making his players better.

The next conversation is with Frans Bosch. His training methods provide context on how we can analyze movement, develop sport-specific training methods, and increase transfer in complex sports such as rugby, American football, soccer, baseball, and more. John Pryor then explains how he has taken the concepts from Bosch and used them to achieve World Cup success with Japan Rugby.

In the final interview, John Kiely explains in-depth the shortfalls of current planning and periodization methods. Rather than turning to technology, his solution is to educate his players so they can take part in providing feedback.

As you will see, all the coaches have a different approach, but they are confronting similar issues and their search for better feedback optimizes the process. In a world where nothing is clear, it is key to learn as much as possible from your immediate surroundings.

8 // DAVE TENNEY

I currently live in Europe, where soccer is a way of life. So when I tell people I am from America, they often make comments about how we don't know anything about the sport. That may have been the case decades ago, but the sport is on the rise in America, and I always give Europeans one example to illustrate that: Seattle Sounders FC. My hometown club is one of the great success stories of North American soccer. The team has an average of over 40,000 spectators per match, higher than the average of all European soccer leagues, as well as many prestigious teams. The team has won many honors over the past decade and, in 2016, won their first ever MLS Cup.

One man integral to the Seattle success story is Dave Tenney. In nine seasons at the club, he worked in a variety of roles including Head Fitness Coach and Sports Science and Performance Manager, before his promotion to High Performance Director. In 2017, he took on a new challenge as High Performance Director with the NBA's Orlando Magic.

In 2015, I watched his staff in action on a trip back to Seattle. Immediately you could see that Tenney combined his academic background in exercise science with an insider's knowledge of the game. Before focusing on sports science, he played the game himself and then was a goalkeeper coach at the MLS level. You have to know the demands of the game before

TRAINING TALK

you can develop a plan to prepare athletes for it. Tenney knows these demands first hand.

After training, we caught up on topics such as addressing sports-specific training in soccer, the role of individualization in a team sport, monitoring and adapting strength programming to the on-field demands of a field sport, and how to close the gap between the US and the world's best.

LESSONS TO LEARN

- Sports-specific work isn't just about the latest and greatest weight room exercise; it is done primarily on the field.

- Strength training for team sports is about finding the optimal compromise after the on-field training is taken into account. This requires flexibility and a keen eye toward the needs of your players.

- Technology can help coaches better track the volume and type of on-field work, thus allowing them to use supplemental training to better fill in the gaps.

TRAINING SPECIFICITY

MB: **To begin, I'd like to quote another interview you did a few years ago:**

> I would say that 80% of the work I would do is fairly specific. It's funny that a lot of people think of "sports-specific," and they think of doing something in a weight room, that may mimic the movement patterns of the sport. I am a strong believer in soccer-specific training, meaning that the athletes spend most of their time on the field, with the proper footwear, using a ball.

With that in mind, how do you go about determining how much specific and how much general work you want to see, and where it is done?

TENNEY: I think there are a couple of different layers to this question. First, there is the weight room component. At some level, you have to acknowledge whether the culture of your sport embraces strength training or not. What we are doing is not just based on what is ideal, but a compromise.

Soccer players are playing year-round in an 11-month season and do not want to embrace weight training as much as American football or Australian football might. We do one main strength session a week and perhaps one to two accessory lifts a week. This is about 20% of our time, but, as I said, that is a compromise. Everything else we do is on the field.

The second layer consists of what we do when we are on the field. This is more specific, although we can split this into generalized work and very soccer-specific work with the ball. I think that coaches often make the assumption that they are training in a "sports-specific" way when in fact they are not. For example you may try to play in smaller spaces, but there the demands of the exercises aren't entirely specific so we may have to consider tempo runs or speed-endurance work over longer distances to supplement it. You can even term that general as well, since it is not with the ball, but it is complimentary to the soccer-specific work.

TRAINING TALK

MB: The whole distinction between general and specific is a bit of a false dichotomy. Exercises are rarely general or specific, but somewhere in between. It is more of a continuum than an either/or situation. Everything is specific in some sense because you are hoping it transfers over to better performance. The question is just how close is that relation. When you say you are doing 80% specific, that means you are doing 80% of the time on the field? And, in general, the work you do on the field is more specific than in the weight room, correct?

TENNEY: It is more along a continuum with what is more specific or more general. I would say about 80% of our time is still spent on the field and that work is more specific, but within that 80% we still do work without the ball, so you'd probably be able to call that non-specific if you want. 20% of the time in the weight room is all considered general work.

The work on the field creates such high volumes of load over the years and careers that it can create strong compensation patterns or impacts on one side of the body or specific muscle groups. We use the weight room work to even that out. Many of our athletes will develop postural problems in the pelvic and hip complex, for example, so we select exercises to rewire them in addition to the strength work. We are doing a lot of single leg work, which we feel has some benefits here; we might do one bilateral strength movement and two unilateral strength movements during our main session. You can argue that every sport is asymmetrical in some way and creates these compensation patterns, and we utilize time spent in the weight room to address this dysfunction and asymmetry.

MB: Distance running coach Steve Magness recently spoke at a Sounders FC strength and conditioning seminar. He has written about conditioning for soccer before, and there was one quote that stuck in my head:

> Don't mimic the sport, but train to be able to increase your ability to perform in the sport. [As an 800-meter runner, I wouldn't] go out and run 800-meter time trials every day be-

cause I'm mimicking the sport . . . We know that we need everything from 60-meter flying sprints and plyo/power work to easy recovery runs and relative longer aerobic work, all in the name of running two laps in under 1:50.

In essence, you don't just train the thing you want to do, you have to work the extremes to find overload that will stimulate adaptations. As hammer throwers, we throw lighter and heavier hammers. Middle distance runners need to train speed and endurance rather than just working in the middle. How do you incorporate this in training and address the different qualities you are aiming for?

TENNEY: One thing we haven't addressed is what the head coach wants from a tactical perspective. So while I completely agree with the quote, I also think we need to layer our approach over top of the training needs of the head coach during the weekly program. We have found there are the things that the head coach really wants to work on, which could result in an overload in some areas and underload in other areas. We can now utilize technology to accurately measure the actual physiological impact of a coaching staff's "training philosophy."

>> **We need to layer our approach over top of the tactical training needs of the head coach during the weekly programming.**

If you think of the continuum from big versus small, soccer players have to be good in very tight spaces in terms of acceleration, deceleration and change of direction, but there is also a maximum velocity element that you have to touch on as well. And then, there is an overall aerobic background as well. Each week we have to decide which one we will focus on. Steve is right; if you just play all the time there is not enough high velocity work, and the heart rates are not particularly

TRAINING TALK

high. You end up with an anterior overload of quads and hip flexors and an underload of max velocity and endurance work. That is the traditional soccer model of consistent small-sided games that are used in training. Again, we are trying to create a training program that balances this out.

You have to see that soccer is a huge volume of sub-maximal work that could be decided by something like maximum sprints. Without addressing that maximum acceleration element and just letting them play, over time the max velocity will degrade. We try to track that with some of our technology to see how much time is spent in those high velocity ranges. If we do not monitor, it is easy for a guy to go two to three weeks without going above 90% of his maximum velocity since he settles into a sub-maximal way of playing the sport.

NEEDS ANALYSIS IN TEAM SPORTS

MB: **How do you go about determining the important traits needed for different players and positions?**

TENNEY: For one, our players wear GPS for most of their pre-season games, and we have a camera tracking system that can measure the work demands. So, we have a pretty good idea of the profile by analyzing the exact physical demands of each position. We have several metrics, such as high speed running which is running at over 5.6 meters/second.

Central defenders, for example, they don't do a ton of high speed running, and they can cover 2 kilometers fewer a game than other positions. These guys will lose some power and maybe some endurance over the season, but you would rather optimize the power and speed over the slight loss of endurance. Compare that to the wide guys we know need to cover 1500 meters to 2000 meters of high speed running in the game and around 12 kilometers total distance in the game; if those guys lose their aerobic endurance, you see a huge drop in their high speed running since they will need too much recovery time between bouts of high-intensity work.

We do have enough data now to see what guys are doing and also measure the fluctuation of performance over the year. If we see sharp declines, we can investigate to see if it is due to loss of fitness, power, or an undisclosed injury. Sometimes it can be as subtle as the guy has picked up a little contact injury (such as an ankle sprain or contusion), and their high speed running drops 300 meters per game. The data helps you see if it is a physical fitness or medical issue.

MB: **I can't help but compare this approach to what I am most familiar with in track and field. As a throws coach, I simply have to determine what we want to train, create a plan, and implement it. You are almost working from the opposite direction. You have to figure out what you want, wait and see what is already done during tactical training, and then create a plan that fills the gaps.**

TENNEY: Exactly. Also as a team sport, we do not have a very homogenous group of athletes. Some are more sprinter fast-twitch types; some are more aerobic slow-twitch types. So you have to see what that training stimulus does day after day to those athletes. Submaximal work may dull the neuromuscular system of the fast-twitch guys a little bit and cause them to lose that pop that makes them dangerous and effective. Whereas, the aerobic guys will eat that type of work up, but if you don't make them sprint, they lose that ability easily, since it is not in their genetic makeup.

I am over exaggerating a little, but typically your wide players can be two different type of athletes. You can have a more aerobic type guy with a miler's physiology. You could have another wide guy who is more like a 200-meter sprinter; he can go, and no one can keep up with him, but he'll need a few minutes before he can go again. The goal with him is to make him a little more aerobic. These two will respond very differently to the training stimulus both daily and long term. What you do with them off the field will modify that, so we pay attention to the long-term effects of sports-specific training in their plan. With the fast-twitch guys we might do some tempo runs or other sprints outside to make sure that

TRAINING TALK

edge is not dulled. What is interesting is the mix of athletes and then what happens to them over the course of the season and their careers as well.

MB: **And further along that point, it is very interesting how the sport has evolved over the last few decades. As strength and conditioning was developing in such team sports, the focus was often just on what happened in the weight room. What you did on the field was a given.**

Now, you can really measure and quantify what you do on the field, and that allows you to better program the rest you do off the field and even optimize the time spent on the field, if you have a good working relationship with the coach. That is a huge step forward because, as you said, most of the work is done on the field. If you are not factoring that into the program, you are ignoring most of the workload put on the athlete.

>> *The technology is allowing the coaches to really understand what the workloads on and off the field are doing to the athletes long-term.*

TENNEY: That's what we find. Now, when we see the high velocity volumes or people sitting around in training, this will impact our strength training programming. And as we get in the season we use things like Omegawave and see how people are tolerating the volumes of the season overall and tailor our strength training to that.

Also, with the technology, we can use that to have a clear communication point with our coaches to make everything fit together. We have a real discussion because we know the volumes and impact of each of their exercises. The technology is allowing the coaches to really understand what hand, there are so many games there isn't enough time to fit that work in. Fatigue is really affecting the quality of the World Cup.

MB: **On the strength and conditioning coach's side, do you feel that the know-how is there and that head coaches are buying in? You were recently visiting Ajax Amsterdam, so perhaps you can compare their approach.**

TENNEY: On the strength and conditioning side, we have a lot of high-level strength and conditioning coaches working in our league. I had a very small minor league career in Germany in the 1990s and have travelled back and forth quite a bit. Overall, the embrace of strength and conditioning is on the rise globally. Culturally, there are some countries that do not embrace it as much. Germany and England have a high number of qualified strength coaches, and in Italy there is a crossover of track and field individuals into soccer, which has brought that strength training culture over. In Spain and Portugal, there is less of an influence.

Across the board, you can see the increase in the facilities and quality of strength and conditioning coaches. And the head coaches that have gone through it and seen the benefits of it are going to push it more. That's what is happening in the MLS. For the most part, 90% of the coaches in the MLS have played in the MLS and see the benefits of high quality strength training. That is happening everywhere.

MB: **With a lot of sports, the hesitancy to do more in strength and conditioning is tied to tradition. They may have had success without it due to a variety of reasons such as their culture, and, therefore, see no reason to change what has worked for them. Up until recently, I've seen that in many Swiss winter sports that we've traditionally succeeded at. It is not until other countries came along and gave them a wake-up call that they started to change.**

TENNEY: I have to be honest too: from a strength and conditioning standpoint, the US is among the best in the world, but there is no winning

TRAINING TALK

games in the World Cup with just physical preparation. Now, we need better and more skillful players. Our academy systems have to be producing more skilled athletes and putting the technical and tactical elements together with the physical elements.

> >> *From a strength and conditioning standpoint, the US is among the best in the world, but there is no winning games in the World Cup with just physical preparation.*

MB: **I guess that is true for many US sports, including the hammer throw. We are definitely not lacking on the strength side compared to the best international throwers, but what is behind is most often the technique and the number of throwers.**

TENNEY: For us, we have younger kids playing in the MLS and World Cup at a younger age like DeAndre Yedlin. He is now in England. We are producing players that are getting opportunities at a younger age, which will aid in their technical development. I think we are following a good path. The integration of strength and conditioning methodology has helped the overall professionalism of US Soccer and development of the professional game here. That being said, from a tactical and technical standpoint, we still have some ground to make up, in order to catch up to the level that other leagues in the world are playing at now.

9 // TOM MYSLINSKI

While America is slowly improving at what the rest of the world calls football, its heart remains with its own version of the sport: American football. The National Football League doesn't just lead the country in terms of fans, money, and talent . . . it also leads the world. No sport can match the number of fans and revenue produced in the NFL. With so much on the line, every tiny detail matters and, as a result, teams have invested a lot in strength and conditioning over the past generation.

Tom Myslinski is a leading coach in this area, currently the head of strength and conditioning for the Jacksonville Jaguars. Myslinki has lived football all of his life. He came to prominence at the University of Tennessee, where he was an honorable mention All-American offensive guard. After college, he was drafted in the fourth round of the 1992 NFL draft and spent the next nine seasons playing offensive line in the league. Since retiring as a player in 2000, Myslinski has continued to work with football as a strength and conditioning coach at both the collegiate and professional level, including work with the Cleveland Browns and the University of North Carolina.

Despite a big focus on football, Myslinski also draws on resources from other sports. As a high school and collegiate athlete, he competed as a thrower, and, as a result, is frequently in touch with track and field coaches

TRAINING TALK

to help refine his program and methods. Like football, track and field is a power sport, and there are a lot of parallels between training for both sports too. Back in 2014 I discussed these influences with Myslinksi and how to adapt them to football. We also continued to cover a wide range of topics including specific strength, sports science, and other variables affecting training.

LESSONS TO LEARN

- Don't just analyze the needs of the sport or the position. Each of the 22 individuals on the field have different needs.

- Consistent loading in weight training provides many benefits. The stable loads allow athletes to focus their energy on the field and also allow coaches to better measure stress and effectiveness of training protocols.

- As football players are subject to high impact and loads on the field, off-field training is more general in nature. Adding a specific weight training program that increases these loads further can be dangerous.

INFLUENCES

MB: **I like to hear about what influences impact coaches. Who or what has been the biggest influence on your approach to training?**

MYSLINSKI: My biggest influence was playing nine years as an offensive lineman in the NFL. I was very lucky; it opened my eyes and taught me, through my failures, a better way of doing things.

Even before that, I was very fortunate to have my dad as a coach. He was ahead of his time. In fact, he played pro football very briefly and was our high school football, wrestling, track, and strength coach. Track was perfect for training for football. I've always believed the throws match up well with football, especially for a lineman; just sprinkle in the aerobic and anaerobic work capacity.

Track and field was a big influence in other ways. We had a very powerful high school track and field team with a lot of throwers moving on to the college ranks. I was fortunate to go to the University of Tennessee where I participated in football and in track and field. My strength and conditioning coach there was Bruno Pauletto, the former Canadian national shot put champion and a guiding light for me.

MB: **I didn't realize how deep your throwing background was.**

MYSLINSKI: Yes, and even in high school, Mike Woicik, who's currently the Dallas Cowboys strength and conditioning coach and used to throw at Boston College, taught me how to throw the hammer. I actually started throwing the hammer when I was probably in 10th grade. He introduced me to the names of Sedykh and Bondarchuk. I was probably one of the few kids in the States that actually knew who they were and admired them.

MB: **Not many people can say that. That's even earlier than I started throwing hammer.**

TRAINING TALK

MYSLINSKI: Later in my career I was lucky to meet my good friend, Buddy Morris, who is now the strength and conditioning coach with the Arizona Cardinals. Buddy was the strength coach at the University of Pittsburgh, when I played for the Pittsburgh Steelers. He really opened my eyes to what was going on. From there, I met Louie Simmons, Charlie Francis, and branched out to meet others and learn ways to fix myself as a player and train more efficiently.

LEARNING FROM THE SOVIETS

MB: You mentioned Bondarchuk already, and I know that some of the Soviet coaches and researchers have been an influence on your training too. Guys like Bondarchuk, Verkhoshansky, etc. What are some of the bigger points you've taken away from them that carry over a lot to American football?

>> *We stabilize and maintain their physical capacities in the weight room so they will grown technically and tactically in the sport they get paid to play.*

MYSLINSKI: Without a doubt, the number one thing is the organization of the training process. Why do we do what we do? It assigns value and gives everything meaning. Let me give you a good example: right now we are in the depths of an NFL preseason training camp, and one of Bondarchuk's big tenets is stabilization of loads. His loading parameters in the weight room stay fairly consistent so the effort is directed to the skill of the sport. Consequently, if you are a hammer thrower your main expenditure is throwing the hammer. So with my guys in the weight room, we realize the most important thing for them is to play football. Therefore, we stabilize and maintain their physical capacities in the weight room so they will grow technically and tactically in the sport they get paid to play.

MB: That definitely makes sense, but you have to admit it is kind of a unique approach. I am probably over-generalizing, but when you talk to a lot of strength coaches from any sport, the focus is often the athlete independent of their sport. They focus on simply getting them stronger or faster, but only indirectly at getting their results better on the field.

MYSLINSKI: One needs to realize that even with this approach the athlete is getting stronger because he is getting stronger playing his intended sport, just like you are getting stronger throwing the hammer. It's the same thing, there is no difference.

MB: **So it's focusing on the type of strength and how you go about it.**

MYSLINSKI: You must control what you can, help stabilize the athlete and his global stresses. If my athletes are exerting maximal speed and strength on the field; i.e. run blocking, taking on blocks, sprinting, jumping, cutting, why do I want to come in and mimic that or add to that physical stress in the weight room, especially when their livelihood depends on it? Then, add in the mental stress because right now, half my guys aren't going to have a job in a month.

> >> *If my athletes are exerting maximal speed and strength on the field . . . why do I want to come in and mimic that or add to that physical stress in the weight room.*

Carmelo Bosco discovered the same thing with the Italian national ski team. He found that as his athletes went through training camp, his athletes actually became weaker in the weight room, but stronger on the slopes, which is the transfer of trainedness you want. That's our goal. We want football players, not weight lifters.

TRAINING TALK

MB: **You are not just training football players though. You are training linemen, running backs, quarterbacks, etc. Each position has different needs. How do you go about trying to identify what the needs of a position and player are?**

MYSLINSKI: We must do a good job of assessing, monitoring, and tracking our athletes' progress. There's a needs analysis of the athlete, of their position, and what's imperative to maintaining their strengths and developing their weaknesses. For example, with the five offensive linemen, the middle three interior linemen are going to be very anterior dominant, much more bulldozer-types requiring a higher amount of absolute strength while the outside offensive tackles, on the other hand, are usually much taller with longer torsos and more rotational in nature.

Our offseason training is initially dictated according to their training background. We'll get 25 rookies and 10-15 free agents arriving every year from different universities or teams, each with a different philosophy and each with a different state of readiness. Therefore, we must find the safest, most productive way to get our athlete fit and customized to the needs of our team. We are more of an up-tempo, zone blocking NFL offense. This style is very popular in high schools and colleges right now. If we were to draft an offensive athlete from the University of Alabama, a more ball-controlling traditional NFL offense, developing their anaerobic work capacity will play a major part in their preparation. There are a ton of situations to consider.

SPECIFIC STRENGTH TRAINING & UTILIZING FEEDBACK

MB: **You mentioned earlier that playing football itself is strength training.**

MYSLINSKI: Absolutely. Every run block is a maximal effort block. One year I had a running back rush for over 1,500 yards in the season and gain eight pounds of lean body mass in the process. Due to some of his physical limitations, his weight room training during the year was directed towards rehab and recovery. I know what you are thinking, but he reported fit upon the opening of training camp.

MB: **How does that impact what you are doing in the weight room then?**

MYSLINSKI: I'm normally only focusing on general training and not sports-specific, especially during the season. The sports-specific work comes on the field.

I also think it's very important to teach from experience and explain why we do what we do and where it relates to the field. For example, earlier today, in a conversation with a young offensive lineman, we discussed the three-point stance. This is foreign to most up-tempo college offenses since they play in a two-point stance most of the time and the art of run blocking is slowly becoming forgotten. We discussed using the ground as a force plate and pushing back into the ground like sprinters push back thru blocks. Then, you are going to brace and stabilize yourself before firing off the ball in order to generate force, much like you do before you start the descent of a squat. It is more general, but you try to get your correlations that way.

MB: **And how else does on-field training affect what you are doing in the weight room with them?**

MYSLINSKI: We are essentially all sub-maximal loading. Rarely, to be honest with you, do my guys go over 85% of their one-rep maximum, even in the offseason. They get stronger through sub-maximal loading. Also, we tend not to change our main training means and methods. It's a much easier way to measure stress; plus, we can see how the athletes respond. If they are approaching us and complaining of sore legs and our loads are stabilized, then I know the stress is not coming from the weight room.

MB: **The consistent loading provides a great backdrop for all those other tasks. If the background is chaotic, you might miss what is going on in the main picture. However without maximum intensity lifting, you miss some of the weight room feedback others feel crucial. What feedback are you using if you are not working up to maximum intensity?**

TRAINING TALK

MYSLINSKI: We use a force plate and measure the power outputs on the bar with an accelerometer. Looking at power outputs relative to body weight gives us a really good reading of their maximal strength levels because we do not test maximal strength throughout the season.

MB: **In throwing, we have it a little easier since our best feedback is how far we throw.**

MYSLINSKI: You have objective measures; we don't. We have subjectivity. When an athlete says they've played a good game, OK, why did he play a good game? Was he playing against a lesser player or a Pro Bowler? Was the athlete in an optimal state of readiness? Was he mentally more prepared for the game? There are so many individual factors. We need to try to create objectivity within a subjective sport. That is very hard.

MB: **There is a lot of discussion of combine numbers and what can be learned from them. Do those numbers mean anything to you?**

MYSLINSKI: If you had asked me that question last year, I would have said no. Ask me that question in another year and I might say yes. Right now I can't give you an accurate assessment because I am trying to figure some things out.

What's clear, though, is that the most overlooked ability is the ability to play the game. I always go back to that aspect. Can you or can you not play football? Generally, looking at those tests, it is a good assessment of their overall physical capabilities. For our new incoming college athletes, we use it as a baseline. When we had a longer offseason, we used the Max Jones quad test on all our athletes, which is a track and field test, as you know.

MB: **The Max Jones test is still popular in the throws: standing long jump, three jumps, 30-meter sprint, and overhead shot put. Even with the combine tests you can see in the big picture if they are strong or fast and go from there.**

MYSLINSKI: Let's look at the 225-pound bench test for reps. This is not an absolute strength test, but the 500-pound bench presser will always do more reps that the 400-pound bench presser. Therefore, you are able to make conclusions on guys based off of their results. If a guy has a 10-foot plus standing broad jump, he's going to have great horizontal power.

SPORTS SCIENCE & OTHER TRAINING VARIABLES

MB: When we were exchanging emails last month, you mentioned that sports science is a big topic in the NFL right now. Can you talk about some of the trends you've seen in that area?

MYSLINSKI: The biggest thing is GPS tracking. We were the first NFL team to use it and are now in our third year of tracking and monitoring our team's training load on the field. It has opened our eyes to the global stress load of the athlete. Everything in training has a price! We are still learning, but it has really helped us plan offseason workouts, develop return-to-play protocols, and understand that the main stressors happen on the field of play.

MB: What are you using GPS to track? Distance covered, speed, directional movement, etc.?

MYSLINSKI: We look at effort values such as different speed ranges, number of sprints in those ranges, sprint distances, accelerations, and decelerations. There are a number of things. You look at different variables for different positions. For example, our outside wide receivers are going to display more top-end speed; they are my sprinters, so their faster sprint values will mean more to me than their slower sprint values. The inside wide receivers, on the other hand, don't always have the ability to get to top speeds so the number of accelerations and decelerations will mean more.

Then it goes back to what we talked about earlier: athlete individualization. I talked about the offensive lineman, but my track and field background has also allowed me to train my outside wideouts like sprinting athletes.

TRAINING TALK

They are my posterior dominant guys. They have to be able to handle the rigors of the high speed sprints. That's where the GPS comes in.

And how can I forget the development of a return-to-play protocol? When we initially got GPS we really used it to view the athlete's requirements on the field. So if an athlete gets hurt, you can confidently guide rehab according to their exact demands before they return to full functional play.

MB: **Yeah. And you're saying for the receivers, sprint training is a huge influence. For your linemen, I'm assuming that throws training is an influence based on your background.**

MYSLINSKI: Yes, to be honest with you I train my big guys similar to shot putters, except adding in the much-needed work capacities. The fitness aspect is enormous. That's where I made a mistake in my own career. At one point, I thought I could do everything in the weight room. Boy was I wrong. I got out there and I realized how unfit I was really quick. I was strong as hell, but I couldn't repeat my power output. That was a valuable lesson in ignorance.

As a 300-pound man, my other major mistake was training as a 100- and 200-meter sprinter; half gassers, full gassers, 110s, and 300-yard shuttles. If I wasn't drowning in lactate, I wasn't working hard enough. So Charlie Francis taught me, "My slow was too fast, and my fast was too slow." Therefore, I unfortunately realized I spent most of my career performing medium intensity training and neglected developing the energy system most important to me: phosphagen. Ever since then it's been the high-low vertical integration approach with our guys.

MB: **Charlie is well known for that in the sprints, but in talking with Derek Evely, we notice this polarization of intensities in the training of best athletes in each track event, from top distance runners to throwers to jumpers. Bondarchuk is another example of this. We tend to throw at a high intensity but are often only around 65-70% in the weight room.**

We're moving the bar fast, but you have to pick your battles and you only have so much high-intensity stuff you can do. Doing it on the field matters most for you, and doing it in the ring matters for us.

MYSLINSKI: I think the big thing the high-low has taught me is the value of recovery and adaptation, the value of alternating your training influences, and how important it is to reset your autonomic nervous system. One day is a sympathetic day, the next day is a parasympathetic day. I will spread the high-intensity load throughout the course of the week, but that really depends on where we are within the training year.

MB: **How is the impact of sports science affecting your day-to-day work?**

MYSLINSKI: I'll be honest with you Martin, our job is really changing. My assistants' roles are so unique and specific. One of my assistants, e.g., is from Australia. I had to find someone that was proficient in using GPS. He's a stud; I'm lucky! I've learned more from him than he probably has from me.

As a strength coach, I have to be involved in the heartbeat of the team so I must be involved all the time. I have to be on the floor, working with them, physically talking to them to get their vibe. I have to be hands-on, but I also have to be able to steer the ship, so at times I have to be up on the deck looking out for icebergs. If I'm below the deck all the time, I can't see icebergs. It's a lot of work trying to be both places. To me, that's what makes my role unique, intertwining everything together. That's why I really rely heavily on my assistants. I put a lot of trust in them.

MB: **One of the issues I see with much of the new technology is that it is gathering lots of great information, but we still need to take the next step and figure out what to do with it. That's the fun part for me.**

MYSLINSKI: It's a learning process for everybody. A lot of it is used for trending and suggesting now. You just can't look at GPS numbers and

TRAINING TALK

know the athlete's state of readiness. You have to also take into consideration that this guy might be rehabbing an injury, his sleep habits, hydration status, if he's been sick, etc. You have to put everything together. That's why I feel it is important to have a data management system and for my own sanity.

OTHER TRAINING VARIABLES

MB: **You have also coached at the collegiate level. What are some of the big differences you see with professional athletes?**

MYSLINSKI: The two big differences that separate pro guys from college guys are their self-awareness and ability to conduct deliberate practice. If we can create self-awareness, they are able to communicate with us better. The better they can communicate with us, the better we can train them. As for deliberate practice, practice means everything to them. It's their job and livelihood. They do not take it for granted.

>> *The two big differences that separate pro guys from college guys are their self-awareness and ability to conduct deliberate practice.*

The three things we preach to our guys are sleep, nutrition and hydration. I want them to control the things that they can control because there is so much in their sport and their lives that is out of their control. For example, we live in Florida and our heat index is 100° F plus every day. Hydration is a big deal here. Our guys must understand that they have to consistently stay hydrated on a daily basis, and that requires work.

MB: **Nutrition has been a big topic for decades now, but sleep has been overlooked for awhile. I don't think it is talked about as much as it should since it has a huge effect on training and performance.**

MYSLINSKI: Cheri Mah is a scientist over at Stanford and has some really good published research on this topic. Her current research concludes that most athletes are about a month in sleep debt. Elite athletes should get eight to 10 hours of sleep a night, but most of them are only getting six to seven. That amount of sleep debt can't be made up through a nap, and has to made up at night.

That's an easy conversation to have with an athlete. "Hey you aren't sleeping enough," and "you need to sleep more," but actually getting it is a different story. That's where the athlete has to learn to be more self-aware and give a little bit too. Maybe the athlete needs to unwire at night, disconnect from the world, and force themselves to go to bed a little bit earlier. They might need to break bad habits and develop new sleep patterns.

MB: **Another big difference for you is how little you actually get to work with your athletes. Does that have a large impact?**

MYSLINSKI: Enormous! How many weeks do you have each year for training: 48?

MB: **For me, it is more like 50 weeks, but it depends on the athlete.**

MYSLINSKI: Yeah, well we have 32, yet another reason why submaximal loading is king. We don't have a lot of time, and as Charlie would say, "The rush to get things done leaves uncertainty down the road."

MB: **That is one of the most interesting things I've heard from your training. You expect football players to be working the highest intensities and really crushing it in the weight room. So your approach is interesting to hear, even though it makes complete sense.**

MYSLINSKI: Ultimately it all comes down to wins and losses. That is what the goal is because that's how we keep our job, if we win games. That is

TRAINING TALK

how we are graded. That is the tough part of our jobs. It is a rush to get things done but a rush to mental maturity. Most of our guys are physical specimens and we just have to clean them up and help them to reach their Ph.D. of sport. That's what I tell them: "When you're in college, you are getting your undergraduate degree. Well, now you're in the pros so you get a Ph.D." To me, the biggest part is simply learning about themselves.

10 // FRANS BOSCH

If you look at the field of training theory, much of the current framework remains unchanged since the 1960s. Despite advances in motor learning, stress science, coordination, transfer of training, and other topics, coaches continue to tack new ideas onto the old framework without rethinking the underlying system. Few have tried to revise or really built on the old model. This is exactly the problem Frans Bosch aims to solve.

Bosch, the former Dutch national high jump coach, has spent the last 15 years building up a new approach that is slowly gaining traction at different levels. He is one of the most innovative minds at work in sport and his more recent book, *Strength Training and Coordination: An Integrative Approach*, add significantly to his approach.

Bosch's continued work is equally rooted in both theory and practice. He is both a (1) a lecturer in motor learning and training theory at Fontys Sports College and (2) consultant to major sports teams like West Ham United and the Welsh and Japanese national rugby teams.

Like with anything new, Bosch's ideas come with a lot of debate, as theory will always precede practice; but even as the practice catches up, there is strong resistance. Just as was the case with Bondarchuk, Bosch has met resistance since he challenges the assumptions we make on topics like

TRAINING TALK

transfer of training. He also brings together new concepts from fields like complex systems theory and motor learning. Whether you agree with him or not, his approach is guaranteed to make you think and analyze how you currently coach.

In this interview from 2017, we focus on several concepts from his latest book including the idea of perfection, the role of variation, and defining movement attractors. Later in the discussion, we also cover transfer, specificity and how these ideas go together with long-term planning and periodization.

LESSONS TO LEARN

- Respect the complexity of movement and training. Human movement is the result of a highly intricate network of co-dependent sub-systems. When a system is complex, training should be trying to bring things together, not take them apart.

- Define the pillars of your technique. In order for movement to respond to the environment, technique needs both fixed elements and changeable components.

- Create adaptable athletes, not adapted athletes. If we create rigid rules that only apply in certain situations, then athletes will fail when they encounter something new. Instead we need to teach the body rules that we can apply in different situations.

PERFECTION

MB: A colleague of mine just attended one of your seminars, and what he found the most interesting were your views on perfection. The mindset of most coaches is that practice makes perfect, and perfection is the goal of practice, but this is not your mindset.

BOSCH: Basically, my idea is that before perfection there is the hurdle of stability. You are from athletics, and I am from athletics; and I am more inclined to believe that stability limits performance before perfection limits performance. Therefore, in training you should not strive for perfection as being the total of the highest possible outputs. Instead, you should try to get movement stability up to a higher level.

If you take high-speed sprinting, perfection might be viewed as the highest force production possible. In training, then, coaches also would aim for the highest force production possible. Stability, on the other hand, takes a look at the bigger picture. If you are sprinting, you are on the ground for $1/10^{th}$ of a second. In that $1/10^{th}$ of a second, there will be errors and the errors need to be compensated. It might well be that the ability to compensate those errors is limiting your force production before you are being limited by the

TRAINING TALK

maximum force production itself. In that sense, it is ineffective to increase force production until you can first control the loss of stability.

> **>> Stability limits performance before perfection limits performance.**

MB: Knowing the goal is one thing, but sometimes, to find it, we have to go in a different direction. In reading about your approach, it seems that in order to stabilize, you need to destabilize the athlete in training. In order to get perfection, you need to seek out their imperfections.

BOSCH: I wouldn't say you try for imperfection, since that would say I would be happy if someone got it wrong or is inefficient. But you have to confront an athlete with instability to stabilize. If you or the environment has no variation, then they are not searching for the most efficient most economical way to perform.

VARIATION IN TRAINING

MB: I guess this is where constraints-led learning comes into play. In chapter six of your book, you discuss three means of introducing variation in training. You can vary the environment, the task, and the organism. A change in the environment might be playing on a different size playing field. Changing the task could be accomplished by changing the foot placement. And, changing the organism could be done by introducing fatigue. Different sports do a better job in some of these areas, but rarely are all three used. Which one of the three do you think is most often overlooked?

BOSCH: The main focus of most coaches is changing the task. That is OK, but changing the environment is a very, very powerful tool. And changing the organism is something that happens under the surface by introducing something like fatigue into the system. What very often is done is that the environment and organism are not put into play. These are much more important possibilities for variation than you think.

If you look at the constraints-led approach, it looks at how each of these three factors constrains the possibilities for successful execution of the skill. There needs to be an overlap in the possibilities of all three. You have to take that into account. There are two requirements for that overlap. First, the overlap has to change all the time. If the overlap is the same again and again, then adaptation will stop. As a consequence of this, there is no one exercise that is a holy grail. Second, the overlap also needs to be small. If the overlap is too big, the task is too easy. That's what you see in most agility drills for field sports: they are too easily compared to the requirement in a game, and they are not challenging enough.

So, what you have to look for is a combination of these three constraints where the overlap continuously changes and is small. Then, the athlete is pushed to the limit, and the task is difficult.

MB: **As with many parts of training, then, it is about finding balance between the different forms of variation. We use variation as a tool for motor learning. But we also use it as a tool for overload. Another point you make in the book is there is always a trade-off when we introduce an overload in training: the more we overload a movement, the less specific it becomes. For example if I throw a heavier hammer, I have more overload, but the movement gradually changes too. Therefore, we have to find the right balance of overload and specificity so that we challenge the athlete, but in a way that is still specific. How do you go about finding that fine line where the overload is too much and becomes counterproductive?**

BOSCH: I think there is no fine line. I do not think that specificity gradually decreases until it is almost zero. I think it falls off the cliff. Let's take the example of running: you use your muscles elastically. If you want to make it harder with overload, you can start running uphill. As a result the elastic component becomes less and, with an increasing slope, it suddenly

TRAINING TALK

has no role any more. At that point, you are better off having long ground contacts and pushing concentrically.

>> *I do not think that specificity gradually decreases until it is almost zero. I think it falls off the cliff.*

With many movement patterns, it is not that specificity very gradually declines until it is almost zero; it suddenly disappears. I am convinced that in something like the hammer throw, as the implement gets heavier at one given moment, the pattern will fall apart, and it is not hammer throwing any more. The environment makes you flip into another phase and another way of organizing the pattern.

MB: That actually makes a lot of sense. Many coaches often have a set rule they use such as, "No implement more than 10% heavier than the competition weight." I prefer to use an eye test when finding the maximum weight an athlete can throw. Each athlete will be different, but the defining factor is that if the movement changes too much, it is too heavy. At a certain point, they start pulling the hammer instead of throwing the hammer. Clearly, there is such a thing as too much overload, but is there such a thing as too much variation in motor learning? We need variation to adapt, but can we do too much?

BOSCH: Actually that is an interesting question. I asked that to Dr. Wolfgang Schöllhorn, who initiated differential learning. He has a graph that shows if there is no variation at all, learning is very low. As you start to vary more, you get better and better results. But if you keep going into more variation, learning goes down again. You have a minimum, a maximum, and an optimal level of variation. My idea is that if you go beyond the differential learning level and vary too much, the knowledge of result (intent) information of the movement goes down, hence learning goes down.

MB: We come back to the topic of balance again and how to balance two extremes. Does that balancing line depend on whether an athlete is training for an open- or closed-skill sport?

BOSCH: Yes, but you cannot undervalue the use of more variation in a closed-skill sport. If you look at what Dutch baseball is doing with their junior pitchers, you see a massive amount of variation, but there is always a target. A lot of the variation comes from changing the environment (e.g. different mound, uphill, down hill, different situations), but always with a target. If you take these three possibilities to vary, then there are a lot more combinations of variation that can still meet the targets and goals of the sports and the limits of variation are not reached that easily.

MB: Throwing the hammer or shot put is a closed-skill sport, and I often run into coaches that do not use variation, as they feel it will hurt the rhythm of the movement. For example, if they throw a heavy shot put, the rhythm is different and will have a negative impact on throwing the real shot put.

My experience is the exact opposite; you develop feeling and a touch through variation. I do not think that it is a coincidence that my most technically strong throwers are also the throwers able to pick up almost any implement and adjust to it rapidly. They just know how to move anything. Where do you think this fear of variation comes from? Is there actually a chance to destroy the rhythm by varying the movement too much?

BOSCH: Only if you change things permanently. If you only throw heavier balls, it will change things negatively. But if you go back and forth, there is not a new rhythm that can replace the old rhythm. It is only that the old rhythm gets more and more information to refine itself.

ATTRACTORS

MB: Let's turn our attention to attractors now. I assume it is in the attractors that you are keeping a close eye on to see when the movement

TRAINING TALK

has fallen off the cliff. The attractors are the pillars of the movement that must remain stable. They are surrounded by fluctuations which can change to help adapt to new situations. If the attractors of a movement stay the same, then one key requirement of specificity is met. But that begs the question: what is an attractor and what is a fluctuation? How do you go about defining attractors for a sport?

BOSCH: If you work in a sport you have never been in before, you first need to look to see if the sport's movements have any similarities to what you know. I am quite convinced that while fast bowling in cricket, sprinting in athletics, and agility in rugby are distinct movements, they have many of the same attractors. So, that is where you start: try to see the similarities.

Then, you can basically run a search program for attractors by looking at key parts of the movement. The attractors need to be in the part of the movement where there is a big time pressure. For example, look for moments where you only have $1/10^{th}$ of a second to get it right. The movement has to be stable and self-organized there, since you cannot change it with feedback in such a situation.

Another place to look is at-risk positions. Take the sport and make a list of all the injuries that can occur. If there is a frequently occurring injury, the system should try and protect that area. The only way to protect that area is to build an attractor there. In this way you have a couple of rules you can use to go searching for where the attractors should be.

MB: **It is interesting that you find so many attractors in common between such different sports. While the coordination for these sports is different, you are saying the basic building blocks are the same, then?**

BOSCH: Absolutely. At this moment, we are doing a course for tennis coaches and we are trying to translate the building blocks from other movement patterns to tennis, and it is not even difficult. We are always finding these building blocks. I made a proposal for these in chapter three, but by no means is it a finished product. That is the next step: we need to find the common stable building blocks for all sports.

MB: This is interesting to hear, since one criticism of your approach I have heard is that it does not include enough general work. Let's put aside the debate about what is "general" and what is "specific" (all training is specific to some degree as we expect it to provide transfer) and focus instead on sport-specific versus sport-generic movements. If you look at your training, what you are saying is that many of the movements you are using are sport-generic. You are actually trying to build a foundation for these athletes by using non sport-specific exercises that can develop attractors in any number of sports.

BOSCH: Just look at what we did with Japan Rugby. John Pryor mentioned this as well in his interview. We did not implement a "specific" speed program. Instead, we worked on these building blocks for agility that can be implemented in all different kinds of skills. Therefore, it has a transferable generic component in there, and the players became quicker without a "specific" speed program.

TRANSFER & SPECIFICITY

MB: Another point I've heard you make in other interviews but that was not focused on in the book as much, is that everything in training has both a positive and negative transfer. We focus on the positive transfer, but the negative transfer might be more important, even though it is rarely discussed. Can you give us an example of how the negative transfer might outweigh a positive transfer in an exercise that has some clear positive attributes in it?

BOSCH: I always explain to my students that if a strength training program or proposal for a strength program doesn't also mention the program's negative effects, it is probably a very poor program. There are many examples of this.

TRAINING TALK

All of these transfers that are seen as positive have to take into account the level of the athlete. For example, somewhere over here in Holland we have a device for the pole vault where you can hang on to it and go into the inverted position, while being lifted some 12 feet. When you go into the inverted position, it can mimic what is happening on the pole.

>> *If a strength training program or proposal for a strength program doesn't also mention the program's negative effects, it is probably a very poor program.*

A friend of mine, who is a pole vault coach, told me this is a very good device for athletes with a best up to 5.40 meters. But, if you do this a lot with athletes at a level of 5.60 or 5.70, there is a negative effect since they are much more sensitive to the rhythm, and the rhythm on this device is not the same on the pole. It has a negative transfer for the rhythm. The negative transfer for the rhythm is not as big as the positive transfer for athletes under 5.40, but for athletes over this level, the negative outweighs the positive. The net positive effect is therefore variable.

Additionally, there are a lot of unproven assumptions about positive transfer. Recently, we wrote an article on the rate of force development. In classic strength training, one of the key claims is that explosive strength training is good for rate of force development. What we did was look at all of the research out there on rate of force development and looked at two aspects: what resistance do they use to measure rate of force development against and why do they use that level of resistance?

We have gone through 270 papers, and only one paper mentions why they use it and what they use. The other papers just assume it doesn't matter, and they use rate of force development in an isometric pull. If you look at literature in other areas, it is clear that rate of force development is not the same against and without resistance. But, we assume one type of training will improve all rate of force development. There are a lot of claims about a "general" transfer which are drawn from very particular, isolated settings.

The transfer claim in training theory has a lot of gaps and jumps to conclusions. Transfer is the most enigmatic thing there is in training.

MB: I always say that transfer is the one thing every coach has in common. We all are aiming for transfer, since we want our training to improve the athlete's ability in their sport, but every coach has a different idea of how to define and measure transfer.

BOSCH: If you look at how specificity is defined in literature, it is an absolute joke. I would say I have the most sophisticated definition of specificity, but it is still at a stupid level of thinking. There should be big thick books on specificity, but there is nothing out there. In that sense, training theory is in its infancy.

MB: How would you define specificity?

BOSCH: In chapter five of the book, I have five categories: inner structure of the movement, outer structure, energy production, sensory, and the intention of the movement, but if you look deeper you could add other categories as well. With enough resources, you could end up with a complicated matrix of specificity, meaning a matrix of how the control system links movement patterns with each other. If we had that matrix, we could easily figure out whether something has a transfer from A to B to C.

I think this work is being completely ignored now. If you look at the research and how they describe exercises used for interventions, the notion of a refined matrix is not even considered. But, at the same time, understanding specificity is the only thing that can bring us closer to what is interesting about training: transfer.

TRAINING TALK

PLANNING & PERIODIZATION

MB: At the start of the book, you speak briefly about periodization and highlight the work of John Kiely in pointing out how science has failed to give us much of a template in this area. One thing that we know about planning is that we need variation, and as we've discussed, a key element of your approach is variation. Is that all periodization is about: variation?

BOSCH: The biggest thing to take into account in planning is the individual variance between athletes. If you want to periodize training, you have to understand how the individual works, which is extremely difficult. You have to know the adaptations that will occur within that individual. It is there that we run into a big problem.

Long ago, I was consulting for British Cycling, and an exercise physiologist there showed me around and showed all of the equipment they had to measure almost anything you could imagine. After the tour, he told me there is only one thing we cannot get a grip on: the adaptations.

Even on a year-to-year basis with an individual analysis, the performance adaptations can be completely different. Staffan Strand showed me his training log for two years back-to-back, and they had the same exact numbers. But, the first year he became European Indoor Champion and jumped 2.35 meters and the other year he struggled to jump 2.20. There was nothing you could find in the training log to explain that. In other words, just writing down what you have done does not give you the adaptations.

From this and from John Kiely's work, it's clear there is no way you can predict the future. All you can do is see what is in front of you and develop a vast set of simple rules to address the problem you are facing in the perspective of a bigger plan.

MB: **So is the focus only short-term, then? Or do you also use a long-term plan?**

BOSCH: I do have a long-term idea of where I want to go, but basically what I have to address now is what I can see now. I was never capable of planning something more than two weeks ahead, since I could not predict where we would be at in two weeks. I have an idea of where movements should be, where the movements are, what are the gang leaders of the errors I should address first, etc. But I can only plan a couple of weeks ahead and then reevaluate where I am at before going to the next step.

>> *I do have a long-term idea of where I want to go, but basically what I have to address now is what I see now.*

LOOKING FORWARD

MB: **Are there any topics that you feel have been overlooked in your book?**

BOSCH: There is always a lot of misinterpretation. One thing people quickly overlook is that the coach always needs to be a good mediator of this stuff. People make a caricature that if you just do these exercises, things will sort themselves out. You still, as a coach, have a difficult task to apply this approach in such a way that the system is under enough pressure to improve. Of all the people I have seen, John Pryor has, by far, been the best at utilizing this with high intensity. He has created situations where these movement patterns are applied under high pressure and intensity, in a way learning will occur. Those coaching skills are essential: applying it in such a way that it is not a simple, boring drill.

If a coach says they have tried this and it hasn't worked, I would say nine out of 10 times, it is because they are not good coaches. This is not a replacement for coaching. It is a tool that the coach needs to be able to tweak and apply to new sports, as Gary Winckler has done in the hurdles and other coaches have done with different sports. It does not take the coach out of the equation.

TRAINING TALK

>> *This [method] is not a replacement for coaching. It is a tool that the coach needs to be able to tweak and apply to new sports.*

MB: **What are some of your current interests looking forward?**

BOSCH: We are looking more at practical application and how you translate this further into practice. In chapter three of the book, you see eight attractors of running, and in chapter seven, you have the prefab idea of movement patterns, i.e. how you can construct from intramusclar to intermusclar coordination to bigger patterns. What we are trying to do now is merge those two ideas into an approach you can use to build up movement patterns.

I mentioned the importance of stability, but look at how little work has focused on the self-organization and stability of muscle contractions. That is an area that could be developed as well. How do muscles organize themselves bottom-up intramuscularly into stable patterns? The hamstring, for example, has a bottom-up function in running, and that is one area we recently published research on.

Hamstrings get injured quite often in running. I am convinced they need to be an attractor in running in a self-organized way. If you agree, then, the next conclusion follows: the hamstring probably needs to be isometric in its optimum length so that it can protect itself. There, you have one building block, and from there, you can go to the next step. If the hamstring works in almost one length, then the knee and hip angle cannot change at will. They are connected with each other (joint coupling). You are already, then, in a bigger picture. Then, continue to zoom out by looking at how you control the trunk, etc. This is an interesting way of starting with anatomy and building up total patterns. The hamstring article just looks at one of these building blocks.

11 // JOHN PRYOR

In the waning minutes of their opening match of the 2015 Rugby World Cup against the powerhouse South Africa, Japan was trailing by three. They were awarded a penalty, giving them a chance to kick and secure a tie. This would have been the safe choice and the one nearly every coach would have made. Instead, they opted for a riskier scrum. This offered a greater upside—the chance for a win—but one wrong move would end in a loss.

For non-rugby fans, the scrum is likely the image of the game you are most familiar with. Eight players from each team pack together to fight for control of the ball. It is a test of strength, patience, technique, and resolve. Japan was under-sized and under-experienced compared to South Africa, but they won the scrum, took the ball back, drove forward, and won the game. Media universally hailed the win as the biggest upset in rugby history. The television announcer even called it one of the most important victories in the history of any sport.

Watching the game, you immediately knew that Japan was doing something right in their coaching and physical preparation. Much of the credit goes to head coach, Eddie Jones, who since then has taken over the helm at English rugby and continued his success there. But, an integral part of the success was also strength and conditioning coach John Pryor. After the game, Jones was the first to credit Pryor for the win by saying Japan's superior handling,

TRAINING TALK

timing, and fitness were thanks to him. As Jones put it, "We can only do that because our conditioner John Pryor has got the lads so fit."

Shortly after the World Cup, I was able to sit down with Pryor, as he travelled through Switzerland with his family. Pryor comes from an athletics background, having competed in the throws and sprints in high school, among other sports. After working on a Ph.D. in biomechanics, he slowly found his way to rugby, and for the past decade, he has been working at the highest levels of the sport, coaching for the Australian national squad, the Brumbies of Super Rugby, and then with Japan. He is currently the head of strength and conditioning for Fiji, and also continues to consult with the Brumbies and the Suntory Sungoliath professional club in Japan.

Throughout his career, Pryor has been an innovator. He was one of the first coaches to introduce GPS technology into training. And, while he was with Japan, he introduced tactical periodization to rugby as well as the innovative concepts from Frans Bosch mentioned in the previous chapter. In our interview, we discussed the details of how he implemented these new ideas and how they influenced Japan's success.

LESSONS TO LEARN

- Prioritize what you want to develop. In rugby, success requires many skills. Define the most important, and design exercises and drills that will allow execution under the changing and complex game situations.

- Skill and strength are very integrated; therefore, skills training and strength training also should be integrated.

- Define how you want to play and build a training program around that. This is the heart of tactical periodization.

SPECIFIC TRAINING FOR A COMPLEX SPORT

MB: One of the things that interests me the most in Japan's preparations for the World Cup was the use of specific training methods. As a hammer thrower, it is quite easy to implement specific training since I have to execute one movement and that never changes. Defining specific is therefore easy. But in rugby you are never truly in the same situation position twice. How did you go about developing such a specific system based on a sport that is so complex?

PRYOR: As a rugby player, what I ideally want is to run in such a way that I have options: I can change direction, I can pass, I can kick, or I can run at high velocity into contact. Having all those options available to you threatens and manipulates the defense.

Several years ago, I developed the idea that physical superiority could only be based on superior acceleration and acceleration consistency (i.e. specific fitness) for the Japanese team, as we are a very small team. I read Frans Bosch's first book, and I thought he was the best guy we could bring in to get involved to develop more specific training systems. Together,

TRAINING TALK

we developed, for the backs, a combination of running and skill at high speed. The big difference with his influence was that rather than traditional speed and agility drills done through pre-programmed pathways, we worked on the concept he calls "options." We want to consistently run well and have all these options available at the same time. If I am running with my legs trailing behind me, for example, I don't have those options. All I can do is make a loose pass to the outside or carry weakly into contact, and the defense can anticipate that.

MB: **How did you then take the options concept and train athletes to be in those positions?**

PRYOR: We looked next at the necessary preconditions for those options. Frans talks a lot about complex systems. The more complex something is, the fewer rules you can have. In rugby, things are inherently complex insofar as you have all these guys moving through space with so many variables. So, we needed fewer rules and developed just two: (1) chest up, and (2) foot from above.

>> *The more complex something is, the fewer rules you can have.*

Chest up creates better abdominal tension, better force transfer and resistance to contact. And, it creates the optimal conditions for better passing. If the chest is not up, I cannot deliver a ball out the back, or I can't provide strong contact, so more options are lost. If the chest is down and the torso is flexed and weak, then we cannot generate the right tension for good passing or optimal contact outcomes.

Foot from above means that if the leg action is trailing behind and the foot is coming to the ground from behind, I can't present the force for a lateral step; and then, one option is already gone.

Then, we tried to create drills that reinforced those two things. In our gym, we had 20 to 30 meters indoors with wrestling mats, and then, I would throw four-centimeter rubber mats randomly on the floor. The variation of the ground surface meant that they might be stepping on the mat or off the mat. If you are running with the wrong leg action over undulating ground, you will trip over and fall on your face. We would make them sprint down the mats and throw a rugby ball or a heavier aqua ball weighing one to five kilos. It is physically impossible to execute that drill without those two features. We did heaps of variations of those drills. I would have the backs race in pairs and have to make these passes. We would use regular rugby balls and aqua balls of various weights to really stress this creation of core tension.

In this way, we moved from teaching drills and giving feedback to developing new drills where the success or failure of the drill is feedback in itself. It moved from extrinsic to intrinsic feedback. Their feedback was if they fell over or moved fast. Or, if they were unable to make the pass at speed, then they probably did not create the necessary core tension. So the players effectively "teach themselves" once these drills are created.

MB: The unpredictability of the drill helps athletes prepare for the unpredictability of the game. What are some of the other variations you used?

> >> *[I]n speed and agility training, athletes are so under stimulated.*

PRYOR: One of the things Frans said to me is that for the most part, in speed and agility training, athletes are so under stimulated. We were just teaching single pre-programmed movements. Anyone can run between two flags. There might be variations in how fast you can do it, but we wanted to develop a more flexible responsive skill set in our players. We wanted to develop fast reactions and fast movements in small spaces.

TRAINING TALK

When you are not training in a high speed and highly reactive way, you will never go to the limit because you haven't trained with the confidence to know that you can put the pass away, so you pass it much earlier. The more work we do in the high velocity, highly reactive zones make our players more confident at playing close to the opposition defensive line.

MB: It's interesting, then, since it not only increases your specific strength or ability to execute certain skills, but as a result changes the whole nature of the game play.

PRYOR: Rugby defenses are so highly organized that you have to make sure the defender does not know what you will do next. If you are running fast and leaning forward, you know I can only make a pass or fall forward. Therefore, I will not attract more than one defender. But, if I come in with the right features, you know a pass could go one direction, or I could step the other direction. Defenders can sense from my body position that I have those options. Then we start to manipulate the defense, once we acquire those physical skill sets.

That was Frans's biggest influence on me. We lost our obsession with linear 20- and 40-meter speed and focused on reaching speed with options. I didn't have quick guys in the first place; you normally need some wingers possible of reaching 10 meters/second to finish plays. Our guys were running 8.5 meters/second, and we were able to get them up to 9.5 meters/second, but that was good enough since they kept the options. And, we did that without any sophisticated approach to linear speed. The options project was more significant because we looked not just at linear speed but catching, passing, and agility speed.

PLANNING & PROGRAMMING

MB: The head coach for the Japan squad was Eddie Jones, who Vern has described as, "One of the 10 best coaches in any sport in the world now." One of the reasons for that is that he had a clear idea of the team strengths and the direction they would go. What was it like working with Eddie?

PRYOR: Eddie is a fantastic coach and was able to articulate exactly what he wanted the players to do. That, then, gave me an exact map of the physical skills sets that I needed to develop in the players. I've never worked with a rugby coach that could give me that kind of detail.

MB: **How was this approach a bit different than other teams you have worked with in terms of the planning going into camp?**

PRYOR: It was different to any team I have worked for. When we assessed our playing squad, we realized that we really did not have any physical advantages. We were smaller, slower, and with only comparable endurance compared to our competitors. But, the Japanese players have a fantastic capacity for enduring hard work. It is part of daily life and part of Japanese culture to endure hardships. So, we knew that we could develop a very tough daily training program and spend more hours a day training than other teams, most likely without the mental burnout that other teams would endure. We would typically train three times every day:

- Headstart training (5:30/6:30 am): Normally not rugby-specific
- Fundamental training (10:00/10:30 am): Rugby units training (scrum, line out, etc.) and integrated strength and conditioning (specific strength, speed, etc.)
- Game training (4:00/5:00 pm): Rugby training and specific strength and conditioning (including activation)

>> *We spent more time on specific skill development than any of our competitors, and we integrated strength and skill completely.*

As you can see, we spent more time on specific skill development than any of our competitors that I am aware of, and we integrated strength and skill completely.

TRAINING TALK

MB: **Another difference is that you had a much longer time to work with the team in camp. Yet, despite having a long time, you actually decided not to use a standard sequential approach to training, but rather a mixed approach. Why was this?**

PRYOR: If you look at our six-month build up, I would have typically started with a whole lot of hypertrophy, then, a whole lot of speed or endurance, and then, pair that back to rugby. Eddie said he wasn't interested in doing that. He wasn't interested in any speed gain I could get that couldn't be seen in his plays. So, right from the get go, we had rugby sessions once or twice every day of the week.

We had to deploy the program with all elements present at all times. We used a three-week cycle and our first block was about 15 weeks. That meant we didn't have the long traditional strength and running build up. We were always integrating our strength and conditioning development with specific skill and tactical development. This probably meant we had slightly less discrete physiological changes (e.g. lean body mass, VO_2, V_{max}), but the changes were more directly transferred to our playing style.

MB: **Would you do it again, even if the circumstances were different?**

PRYOR: If I had the chance again, I would have done it the same way. The gains in strength, as measured in the gym, were certainly less than with a traditional approach, but the application and transfer were enhanced significantly.

Initially, I found it frustrating because as a strength and conditioning coach, you like to have those longer periods of uninterrupted strength and running development. But, you need to make yourself accountable to the rugby program. My opinion on it now is completely different than what it was on the past. We made smaller more gradual gains that were more directly transferred to the field.

I took some risks in this preparation. For example, none of our backs did any traditional lower body strength training for six months. No squat, no deadlift, no cleans. I don't think any other team at the Rugby World Cup would have done this, though I am not certain.

> **>> We made smaller, more gradual gains that were more directly transferred to the field.**

We invested in much more movement-specific exercises and focused on "skill with resistance" rather than strength exercises that are really just borrowed from other sports, such as taking the clean from Olympic lifting and squat from powerlifting.

MB: As an outsider, I wonder why more team sports do not take this approach. When you train the qualities together, they just fit together easier. When you train them separately, it is harder to transfer from one to another and you develop more imbalances. For example, in throwers, I see many do long strength phases but then, never put those gains back into the throw. Since they neglected their technique so much during that stretch, it sets them back tremendously, despite being stronger.

PRYOR: If a 67-meter hammer thrower took that traditional step periodization approach, how much would their results fluctuate during the year? 10 meters? That just doesn't make sense to lose so much. I was coaching sprinters before, and I would have 10.3 guys. If I knocked on their door in the winter, they wouldn't be able to break 11 seconds. But, they were strong. I was getting them strong in winter, but damaging their speed, and thus, the training was not specific and not right.

MB: **And more to that point, if you do everything at once, you are never**

TRAINING TALK

far from your best. That means your timing is on, since you are learning skills in the same state you will play in.

PRYOR: Timing is one of the most important things in rugby. Executing these complex back line plays requires timing. Not every team needs these plays; South Africa can send out single runners, and they have the strength and size to get over the gain line. We didn't have that option, so we were completely reliant on quite complicated plays to manipulate the defense to get over the gain line. That meant timing was everything.

If I had some guys who were a little fatigued and their speed was not there on a day when another player's speed was there, then we cannot develop those plays. Hence, the need for that type of periodization and also weekly tactical periodization.

Eddie would know with 100% confidence that I have prepared the guys to run their fastest on Tuesday, and there would be nothing to interfere with the skills he wanted to deploy at that training session. We would try and do that twice a week. On other days, we would accept some level of residual fatigue. Those would be the physical days focused on contact and scrummaging.

TACTICAL PERIODIZATION

MB: **You mentioned tactical periodization, and that is a buzzword lately in field sports. Can you describe tactical periodization in one sentence?**

PRYOR: I do not regard myself as an expert, but Eddie and I certainly researched tactical periodization and, then, applied it to our situation. It is a prioritization of qualities based on a tactical rather than physiological model. So, when Eddie says this is the way he wants to play a game and we need to play it that way every Tuesday, then we prioritize those qualities on a tactical basis.

Before that, our whole periodization model was based on physiology. We might want to do more aerobic work here or more strength work there, but with tactical periodization, we instead focused first on tactics/team organization. The model's fundamental underpinning is the tactical game plan. It dictates how the whole week is set up.

> **>> The model's fundamental underpinning is the tactical game plan. It dictates how the whole week is setup.**

MB: **Can you give some examples of how that would have changed your day-to-day preparations?**

PRYOR: The biggest impact was in the matching of training sessions. It is how you prioritize the elements within that day. On a Tuesday, Eddie might say the 11:00 am skills session is the most important session; he wants to run skills at absolute 100% speed. So, anything I do at the 6:00 am session needs to complement the 11:00 am session and not take away from it. It doesn't mean you only do those things. The third session of the day, I might be able to do something more fatiguing or strength-based. But, the prioritization for that day and the sequential days are based on his requirement and the team's tactical requirements. If the skill work will be focused on line-outs and that does not need to be done at anything more than 90% physical freshness, I would have more options. Before, I would dictate the week based on what the physiological demands of our strength and conditioning.

12 // JOHN KIELY

If you read most traditional textbooks on periodization, they are laden with scientific terms and explanations. But if you look in detail at the footnotes, often very little practical research has been done. Theories and anecdotes become facts without the application of science's critical eye. In other words, the planning methods we have been taught have no foundation. This is a pet peeve that Irish coach John Kiely does not mince words about.

Kiely first came to my attention after I read his 2012 article, "Periodization Paradigms in the 21st Century: Evidence-Led or Tradition-Driven?" in the *International Journal of Sports Physiology and Performance*. The article provided a critique and a way forward for periodization.

As Kiely explains in more detail below, he lives with one foot in academia and one on the field (as well as the track). His practical background includes work with the Irish National Rugby Team, working as head strength and conditioning coach for British Athletics, and helping world champions like triple jumper Phillips Idowu and squash player Laura Massaro.

Kiely earned his master's in sports performance and continues doctoral work while teaching the next generation of coaches as a senior lecturer at the University of Central Lancashire. This background has given him a great perspective on the sport in a way that pure academics and coaches don't get.

TRAINING TALK

In our training talk in 2015, Kiely went into more detail about the scientific shortcomings of modern periodization. He also provided a way forward with some suggestions on what we can take from science and tips that help us improve the process rather than focusing on the plan.

In addition to bridging theory and practice with track and field, this interview provides a nice conclusion to this book as it reinforces one of the main topics we keep coming back to. You will have found some examples of training in this book, but you will not find a training plan because it is not about the plan. The focus is on real coaches and the process they use to develop champions again and again. Each coach I have interviewed has a clear process and philosophy that influences their training methods. It is this process, and not the plan, that is to credit.

LESSONS TO LEARN

- Despite the rhetoric of periodization gurus, we cannot scientifically prove that one periodization plan is better than another. Study design has its limitations and cannot be easily adapted to test long-term training methods.

- It's about the process, not the plan. Training is complicated by innumerable variables, and no plan can adequately account for it all. No matter how good the plan, these variables always exist. The best plan is having a process to deal with the variables. This requires flexibility and the willingness to admit the limitations of our knowledge.

- Athletes need to believe. The best program will not work without athlete buy-in. And, a mediocre program can produce great results with faith. Get your athletes involved in the process so that they take ownership and buy in.

THE SHAKY SCIENTIFIC FOUNDATIONS OF PERIODIZATION

MB: **I came across your name when reading your article,** *"Periodization Paradigms in the 21st Century: Evidence-Led or Tradition-Driven?"* **A great point you made was about how shaky the scientific foundations of periodization are. Why is there such a disconnect between science and periodization?**

KIELY: Firstly, and most obviously, the periodization problem is a confusingly complex long-term development puzzle. In contrast, academic training studies are inevitably simplistic, group-based and short-term.

In a sense, trying to piece together a comprehensive periodized philosophy, using available evidence, is like looking through a keyhole and trying to describe the outside world. We get imperfect, incomplete, potentially misleading snapshots. But because these are all we have, the overriding temptation is to construct grand all-encompassing philosophies around woefully incomplete information. And, in the published periodization literature, this is exactly what's happened.

TRAINING TALK

Suppose I've just devised some new means of organizing training and want evidence to support its validity. I access a population of athletes; I divide them into two groups; I change the training of one group (according to my new design); and four weeks later, I evaluate who has improved the most. Now, unless my new design is outrageously bad, the group who received the novel training stimulus will demonstrate the greatest improvements, not because there is something magical in the new design, but simply because the new arrangement of training provides a temporarily novel adaptive stimulus.

Have I proven my design is better? No, I've just shown that change is a potent stimulus to spur adaptation. After some continued exposure to the same program, the law of diminishing returns kicks in, and progress inevitably slows. If, then, you were to reinstate the original program, gains would again temporarily accelerate.

Unfortunately, studies like this are commonly interpreted as validating specific training designs, when in reality they only serve to illustrate the value of regularly varying training: the value of constantly seeking new triggers to nudge the neuro-biological system towards better sport-specific fitness. But, this isn't the end of the story.

Even if we could establish a "best" training design over the four-week period, this doesn't automatically mean that repeatedly varying training in this way every four weeks is the best long-term strategy. It seems much more likely that persistent "variation" (in terms of repeatedly altering training stimuli) is the best route to short-term improvement. But that "consistency" (in terms of repeat exposure to a limited core of performance-specific stimuli) is fundamental to ongoing long-term improvements.

Inevitably, optimal training organization demands that this negotiation, between variation and consistency, is astutely balanced. If variation is too frequent and too broad, then training stimuli are too widely dispersed, and positive adaptation is too thinly spread. Alternatively, if there is too little variation, then the athlete is exposed to the negative consequences of training monotony: diminishing returns, overuse injury, over-reaching, burnout, staleness, decreasing motivation, and so on.

As a further complication, while a sudden change in applied training stimuli may be the quickest route to short-term performance improvements, sudden change also dramatically escalates the risk of breakdown and injury.

In essence, appropriate training management is about resolving paradoxes. There is a balance to be negotiated between variation and consistency; between volume and intensity; between imposed fatigue and fitness reward. Unfortunately, conventional periodization dogma doesn't acknowledge this reality. There's a lot of discussion about how to sequence training modalities, when to change (in terms of training phase duration), but it's all very dictatorial in nature and offers little meaningful insight.

EGOS & GURUS

MB: **In addition to the lack of a way to easily verify training methods, it is also an area where gurus are all over the place.**

KIELY: I totally agree. The periodization literature is a battleground of personalities and is historically dominated by competing egos. In a sense it's, "eminence-based" rather than "evidence-based."

In 1978, Matveyev detailed his philosophies in his little green book *Fundamentals of Sports Training*. This was translated into English in 1981, and because it contains "Soviet secrets," we all rushed to embrace it. But, it's practically unintelligible. I totally respect the amount of work and effort it took to compile, but reading it is not unlike reading Nostradamus; it's so vaguely expressed, using such esoteric and undefined terminology that you can take any message you like from it. Yet, this is the book held up as the epitome of Soviet sports science, as scientific justification of the periodization principles that constituted one of the great secrets of Soviet success.

TRAINING TALK

But it's clearly not a science book, it's a story book: one man's commendable, but deeply flawed, attempt at synopsizing a bewilderingly broad range of phenomenological behaviors, using data collected in the 1940s and 1950s, interpreted through the scientific lens of the 1960s and 1970s.

Subsequently, Yuri Verkhoshansky, who had an intense rivalry with Matveyev, attacked him. Then, more recently, Issurin slams first Matveyev, then Verkhoshansky, explaining why their ideas are "wrong," before using the same dodgy deductive reasoning and selective interpretation of limited evidence to substantiate his personal position and periodization product.

> >> *Major periodization theorists essentially promote the importance of the plan, at the expense of the process.*

In truth, the planning philosophies of these three theorists have more commonalities than distinctions. Each builds a planning philosophy upon a foundation of flimsy evidence and biased simplistic reasoning; each offers a formulaic set of universal planning rules they suggest can be meaningfully applied in different contexts; each underestimates the importance of prior training and individual differences in regulating how athletes will respond to future training. Ultimately, each constructs a storyline marketing their individual interpretation of the "best" periodization template.

Critically, and this goes for all the major periodization theorists, each essentially promotes the importance of the plan, at the expense of the process. Each focuses on foretelling what should happen, rather than focusing on how best to manage what actually happens, which seems, to me, a completely back-to-front perspective.

MB: **Earlier, you talked about some of the research on periodization and how it falls short. But, even worse is that many theories don't even take** that first step and just work off of assumptions without any evidence as to why we should accept them.

KIELY: The deeper I've looked at the "science of periodization," the more I've come to realize that it doesn't really exist in any substantial form: it's an illusion, a fable. Essentially, what we've done is pieced together sporadic snippets of information, structures from conventional social planning models and the occasional academic study, to construct a convenient belief system. A belief system, which a couple of decades ago, helped us to structure training plans, but now, at least in my opinion, is standing in the way of progress.

Further clouding already murky waters is the cultural reverence we hold for Soviet sports science. Soviet training theories still provide the theoretical backdrop for a lot of current practice. And I think that this is, in large part, because we're still impressed by the illusion of Soviet sports science and Soviet training methodology.

>> *The deeper I've looked at the "science of periodization," the more I've come to realize that it doesn't really exist in any substantial form; it's an illusion, a fable.*

What the Soviet Union did very effectively was mobilize populations of children to actively partake in physical education and organized sports; establish coaching as a respected profession with education pathways and career progressions; reward effective coaches; and retain experienced ex-athletes as coaches. Crucially, in a society where opportunities for success were scarce, generations of Soviet kids were given both the opportunities and motivations to engage in physical activity and commit to structured, long-term sports development programs. And, obviously, as we all know, there were other, more sinister contributors to Soviet success.

TRAINING TALK

My point is, we've tended to mindlessly accept that, as the Soviet sports machine was highly successful, Soviet sports science and planning theories were similarly exceptionally good. I don't think that's the case. More to the point, I think we need to stop accepting these historical training philosophies based on what is, for me, mythology.

From a periodization perspective, there's a glaring irony here. If you look at Soviet social planning philosophies, such as their five-year plans, they were a complete disaster: ineffective; inefficient; costly; tragic in terms of human suffering; ridiculously exposed to the unexpected consequences inherent when you impose simplistic rule-based decision-making on deeply entangled complex phenomena. And, consequently, such paradigms have rightly been confined to the dustbin of human planning theories. Yet, we still reverently talk about Soviet sports training planning, which is essentially just a thinly veiled version of Soviet social planning theory applied to training contexts. Go figure!

So, putting this together, we get a blend of complex phenomenon, rudimentary scientific understanding and the influence of an overly-simplistic social planning philosophy. Out of this convergence of influences pops our conventional periodization theories, as represented in the published literature.

IT'S ABOUT THE PROCESS, NOT THE PLAN

MB: **Having worked for a long time with a Soviet coach, I obviously am a bit biased on any discussion of Soviet training methods. But to Bondarchuk's defense, these are many of the criticisms he launches on other Soviet greats, and what makes his approach different than the standard Soviet approach is that it is based on the process and not the plan.**

KIELY: Certainly your experience supports what I've heard about Bondarchuk's training. He readily adapts the plan in response to emerging information so as to exploit opportunities and detour around threats. That adaptive mindset—always observing, always ready to respond—is, to my way of thinking, a fundamental dimension of solid coaching.

But, crucially, when we look back on what's been written about periodization, and especially when we look at the most widely read publications and theorists, it's the plan that's promoted; it's the plan that's debated; it's the plan that's persistently highlighted. Whereas the process—the need for the coach to be tuned in and alert; the need for the coach to be a creative problem-solver; the need for the coach to be responsive to emerging challenges; the need for the coach to nurture athlete "education;" the need for the coach to be sensitive to "weak signals" heralding growing risks and vulnerabilities—is persistently undervalued.

Most young up-and-coming coaches haven't worked closely with a coach of Bondarchuk's stature, and consequently, won't have witnessed firsthand how he might manage and adapt the plan. Most coaches, instead, will turn to what's been written and the messages presented in coaching seminars or education workshops. And, these messages haven't changed much over the past two or three decades.

Think I'm exaggerating? The educational programs of the world's foremost S&C body, the NSCA, still cite Selye's early work on stress from the 1930s as providing a logical foundation for periodization concepts. The fact that Selye's early theories, suggesting a universally-shared adaptive trajectory, have long been upturned, recalibrated and rewritten is conveniently ignored in favor of presenting the illusion of a seemingly scientifically supported storyline.

My problem, in a nutshell, is the presentation of convenient opinions masquerading as evidence-led conclusions. If you have an informed, experience-led, carefully thought through perspective, great! Let's talk. I'm all ears. If you want to convince me that your periodization "product" is the best using woo-woo pseudo-science, "Sorry, my brain is too small, and my life is too short." So, I don't think we should endlessly regurgitate poor logic and poor science. In fact, I feel the majority of what's been published on periodization is actually obscuring our vision and getting in the way of proficient training management.

TRAINING TALK

There are now so many competing brands of periodization—conjugate sequence, fractal, non-linear, reverse, block, etc.—that we're culturally stuck in debates and arguments about which is the best system. Even worse, we're stuck in the mindset that there is a best system. But the reality is that constructing a storyline supporting each method; providing a veneer of academic support; pointing at high-achieving athletes or teams who used similar planning constructions, is child's play. And, for me, that's a fundamental limitation of how we think about periodization.

MB: **Another shortfall I see of many Soviet periodization theories as that the theories have spent more time being debated in the classroom than on the field. As a coach with experience both in the classroom and on the field, how do you see that?**

KIELY: In reality, in elite environments, effective planning isn't about constructing the perfect plan; it's about making your best possible guess at what should work, but doing so in the expectation that this plan will be tweaked and evolved in response to emerging information. From this perspective, sticking to the plan religiously isn't a virtue. Consistently turning up in the best possible state of mind and body and making an informed decision on how best to target technical quality, volume and intensity to most appropriately move you towards realizing your goals, on the other hand, is.

When you look around you see that there have been many, many coaches, past and present, who didn't buy into the logic of regimented planning: thoughtful, experienced practitioners who saw through the mythology, who saw the Emperor wasn't actually wearing any clothes. But these coaches weren't professors dodging behind archaic terminology and citing inaccessible or untranslated academic evidence, and consequently, these coaches aren't well represented in the published literature. They were busy: coaching, guessing, observing, tweaking, learning from mistakes.

Encouragingly, although the academic perspective on periodization is stuck in a Soviet-dominated time warp, the practical world is moving on. Social media is providing experienced practitioners with the platform to share thoughts and ideas. Historical edifices are crumbling. Thoughts that not too long ago might have seemed wildly heretical, are gaining traction. It doesn't matter that we all have different interpretations and opinions, the important thing is that we're endeavoring to put in the hard yards to move our planning cultures forward. I'm looking forward to seeing how our planning philosophies evolve in this new, and hopefully guru-free, era.

MB: **We've spent a lot of time on this topic. If you had to sum up this discussion in a few words, what would you say?**

KIELY: If I was to summarize briefly: I think periodization paradigms were historically useful. They reduce confusion and cognitive dissonance, the discomfort of thinking deeply about paradoxical questions. Pre-formulated periodized structures provided us with a map that helped us navigate a confusingly complex and unknown terrain. But now, I feel, they've outlived their usefulness and we need to move on. I think they obscure conceptual clarity and they inhibit philosophical understanding.

When we believe in non-existent "rules," we are not as alert as we should be. Our imagination is not as open to possibility as it should be. Our thinking is overly-formulaic, and our problem-solving agility is bound by imagined theoretical constraints. And, I don't feel that's the most effective route for us to attain planning wisdom and guide the athletes who place their trust and hope in us.

MB: **So what can we do?**

KIELY: We have to face up to reality, face up to what we don't know. We can't over-simplify, yet we can't throw our hands up at the overwhelmingly complexity inherent in the planning problem.

Perhaps we need an approach that simply acknowledges it's bloody hard. Get stuck in. Do your best in the certain knowledge you will make mis-

TRAINING TALK

takes, but design your process to make sure you learn from those mistakes. Every situation and every individual athlete is inevitably unique. Take your time; think deeply; design your plan. But as importantly, design your process to be sensitive to emerging information. Be meticulous in your preparation; put your heart into formulating your plan, but be ready to tear it to shreds once you become too attached to it. Once your planning paradigm starts to limit the scope of your vision, automate your thinking and diminish your openness to possibility.

>> *Be meticulous in your preparation; put your heart into formulating your plan, but be ready to tear it to shreds once you become too attached to it.*

THE IMPORTANCE OF CRITICAL THINKING

MB: So far we have been discussing the shortfalls of science in the tackling periodization. But many of these issues are broader than science, aren't they?

KIELY: When we think of science, we automatically think of academia. But academia is just another institution, as riddled with egos and small-mindedness and dull convention as any other human collective.

But scientific thinking, perhaps critical thinking is a better term, is something separate, something purer. Certainly, it's imperfect, but it is the best tool available to aid us in progressively uncovering more accurate approximations of reality.

Critical thinking is a process: a problem-solving style, a clinical approach, and an ego-neutral mindset. It's not dispassionate and cold and robotic; it's the product of passion and intensity and effort. I think of it as simply the logical and unbiased search for clarity. A clarity that comes from careful consideration of available information—where information comes in many forms: evidence, experiences, observations, and so on. I shouldn't believe you because of who you are, what you are, what you have achieved in the past, or because your stance happens to agree with mine. I should believe you only if you provide a rational means of explaining the evidence, a means that sheds more light on a particular phenomenon than previously available.

I know coaches with little formal education who naturally adopt a critical thinking style. Likewise, I know the most educated of academics who will never have an original thought; who can't express an opinion without referencing someone else's previous work; who seem to be, metaphorically, facing backwards into the past, rather than forwards into the future.

Similarly, I know coaches who base their training programs on tradition and hand-me-down anecdotes, are adamant in the validity of their systems, and are resistant to criticism yet never question why they do what they do. And, scientists who are artistically creative and innovative, and as they learn, continually demolish and re-build their belief systems accordingly.

The cry in the coaching world of, "But this is the way we've always done it," is the mirror image of the academics cry, "But such-and-such proved it." Both appeals display a hint of desperation; both reflect the same philosophical insecurity.

MB: **With that being said, how can science help us better understand the periodization and planning problem?**

KIELY: Most obviously, we get snippets of insight from training studies. But that's all they are, snippets: in this specific context; with this specific group; if we perform this specific type of training; then, this is the likely averaged outcome. Such studies don't prove anything. They make a suggestion. And if you look closely enough, you see such suggestions are often contradictory.

TRAINING TALK

In relation to training organization, for example, many studies (starting with Hickson's classic in 1980) have "proven" that mixing endurance and strength (or power) training causes an "interference effect," diminishing the gains you would expect if you solely executed one form of training. Since then, similar studies, across a range of training modalities and ability levels also suggest that simultaneously performing multiple forms of targeted training—endurance, strength, and so on—sometimes cause interference, sometimes result in no inhibition, and sometimes result in synergistic, beneficial consequences. Are some of these studies wrong, and some right? No, they all reflect the specifics of the particular design: the level of athlete; duration; training particulars; measurement tools, and so on.

The study results are the study results. All they prove is that in this artificially constrained, very specific context, when we did this that happened. They don't prove the worth of a particular training model. You can choose to believe the studies supporting your perspective (and reject the ones that don't); or you try piece together a logical conclusion—from all these various jigsaw pieces—that coherently fits current evidence. So, training studies help us shine a light, but can't solve the problem.

MB: **In relation to periodization, what are the other impacts of the study design?**

KIELY: Conventional training study design typically goes something like this: measure some dimension of fitness; introduce a specific form of training for a limited time span; subsequently re-evaluate the fitness measure of interest. If the experimental group significantly improved fitness, then the study authors would conclude that 'X' type of training improves 'Y' fitness measure. What they really mean, of course, is that when all individual gains and losses are averaged, the resulting averaged fitness score of the group significantly improved.

If we look at modern studies investigating how individual participants, rather than group averages, respond to training, we see a very large spread of adaptive responses. We find sluggish adapters, super-adapters and everything in between. And, although we always knew people vary somewhat in their responses, we didn't truly appreciate the scale of inter-individual differences. In short, adaptive responses are widely dispersed, not tightly grouped, around the average response. To that extent, the average is not necessarily reflective of any individual response.

In the same sense, if you summed the heights of an NBA and a junior school basketball team and divided by the total number of players, you would, of course, get an average height, but it would not necessarily be reflective of the height of any one individual. The implication is that you can't look at someone and know how they will respond to any applied training stimulus.

>> *[A]daptive responses are widely dispersed, not tightly grouped . . . the average is not necessarily reflective of any individual response.*

In a very real sense, conventional planning dogma assumes training adaptation conforms to stereotyped trajectories and that the magnitude of improvement is largely predictable. And, if we can't even predict how individuals will respond to the straightforward unidirectional training stimulus such as a basic strength or endurance program, you certainly can't accurately forecast the consequences of typical sport training programs involving multiple forms of training overlaid in complex mosaics.

LEARNING A NEW WORLDVIEW

MB: **If the training science cannot easily solve the problem, where else can we look for evidence to help?**

KIELY: Here's the thing: I don't think we understand something simply because we know lots of related facts. I may have my head stuffed with snip-

TRAINING TALK

pets of information, but unless I have a coherent paradigm—a framework for understanding how the particular phenomenon works—I can't make sense of how these isolated observations fit together.

Once, we thought the Earth was flat and positioned smack in the center of the universe; this explanation fitted the available evidence. But, then, we learned new facts that this paradigm could not coherently explain, and a new belief system better fitting the facts emerged. There was a paradigm shift. So, accumulating scientific insight gradually changes how we think, changes how we perceive and, consequently, how we seek to solve problems. In essence, accumulating snapshots, from across scientific domains, gradually merge to shape our perception of how the world works.

As another example: up until 50 years or so ago, the conceptual lens through which we viewed observable behaviors was mechanical in nature. Newton had reduced the physics of universal motion to a set of linear equations; Harvey depicted the heart as a mechanical pump; Descartes described the human body as a machine. The hidden message, embedded in these philosophies, was that we functioned in a predictable, automated manner. Our bodies were merely fleshy machine parts, manipulated by our brains for fuel and transport. The logic then followed: if you know the rules, you can determine the future. If you know the formula, just enter the numbers, and a predictable answer will pop out.

But, gradually this worldview changed, and in turn, it has changed how we perceive the "rules" of athletic training. Beginning in the abstract world of mathematical physics at the end of the 19th century—with plenty of detours along the way—we've gradually transitioned from a linear worldview to one that is inherently non-linear, chaotic, and complex. The people who drove this conceptual revolution surely never considered how their work might influence athletic training, but it has. And, it has by reshaping the paradigms through which we view the world. Am I exaggerating? Maybe, but I don't think so.

Take traditional training lore. If we look at conventional dogma, as expressed in the most widely read and recommended text books, what do we see? Linear logic. This number of sets, for this number of repetitions, at this intensity, will give you this result. First train for size; then for strength; then for power. First for endurance; then for speed. Really? Seriously? How suspiciously convenient. Convenient because it allows us to wrap up our training plans within linearly organized structures. This is a prime example of not letting the truth get in the way of a good story.

It's not that such designs are not valid or won't work. For many athletes, of course, they will. Within reason, if you train consistently, regardless of structure, you will get better. But simply getting better is not the goal of optimal training design, is it? Again, the issue is that the linear logic underpinning many traditional assumptions blinds us, leads us to believe there are set rules, when really there are wide-ranging better or worse possibilities.

There's a lovely term summarizing this phenomenon: path-dependence. Path-dependence describes when a belief-system, practice or habit emerged to solve a historical problem, but then persisted after the original problem vanished.

MB: **I see that in my office all the time. We have so many processes we follow, simply because that is how we have always done them. Although, who knows if some of the processes ever solved a problem in the first place?**

KIELY: The classic example is the QWERTY keyboard. You probably know the story. When the typewriter was first manufactured, the QWERTY arrangement slowed typing speed so the mechanical mechanisms wouldn't jam and also because it allowed unskilled salespeople to demonstrate the efficiency of the new tool by easily typing the word typewriter, the letters of which are all on the top row of keys. But, now that the problem of mechanical jamming has vanished, surely there's a more ergonomically

TRAINING TALK

efficient way we could design keyboard lettering. The benefits of positive change seem obvious; but, change is hard.

The more we do something, the more that habit becomes institutionally fossilized. Doing things the way we've always done them becomes the path of least resistance. In the case of keyboards, the resulting costs, chaos and upheaval of any retooling are mind-bending.

I think, culturally, we suffer a path-dependent blind spot in periodization. We acknowledge we live in a complex and chaotic universe; likewise, we acknowledge our biology is complex and chaotic. Yet, we still adhere to this clunky, unreflective of reality planning belief system. Culturally, if we were to sift through conventional practices, we would uncover many instances where we're living with path-dependent relics of the past; practices that are resistant to change purely because that's how we've always done it; practices that have gradually become ingrained in our psyches; and it's become easier to keep doing them than to stop.

When we lived in our old reliable mechanical universe, our periodization assumptions made sense, but now that our understanding of how the world works has moved on, stubbornly sticking to these beliefs seems like willful blindness.

MB: **Can you give an example of how a changing worldview or refined scientific insight has affected your own personal approach and philosophy?**

KIELY: Consider this question: how good are human "experts" at predicting how the future will unravel? It's a simple question, yet difficult to evaluate.

When we think of phenomena such as human health, physical training, financial markets, industry, politics, warfare, and economics, each seems very different to the next. But, all share a simple, single overarching feature. All are complex adaptive systems, systems comprised of multiple component sub-systems interacting in inherently non-linear and chaotic ways. Such systems are sometimes resilient to cataclysmic trauma, yet sometimes vulnerable to minute disturbances. Sometimes the crippled plane safely lands on a single engine; sometimes an ill-fitting washer brings down a space shuttle.

Culturally, we've lived through the recent financial downturn. I dare say we've all experienced the gut-wrenching realization that an athlete has just injured himself. Maybe these two phenomena are not as philosophically unrelated as we might think?

Was it a few greedy individuals who brought financial hardship upon the rest of us, or was it a systemically corrupt culture already teetering on the edge of collapse, just waiting for the wrong nudge, at the wrong time, in the wrong place? Was it that last step that tore the hamstring? Or the integrated consequence of accumulating fatigue interacting with the legacy of a past trauma, interacting with a shift in attentional focus, resulting in an inaccurate activation—a coordinative error ultimately resulting in a momentary overloading of a handful of fibers?

Because complex adaptive systems adapt, re-routing how they operate to successfully achieve equivalent outcomes though a multiplicity of routes, complex chaotic systems are commonly robust to insult, far more robust than mechanical systems. It's why humans have not only survived, but thrived. We are adaptable. We roll with the punches. But, if a complex chaotic system is sufficiently finely balanced, poised on a metaphorical knife-edge, then one homicidal butterfly intent on meteorological Armageddon wreaks havoc.

So, let's accept that there are certain common core characteristics across complex adaptive phenomena. The systems are obviously not the same, but they certainly have more similarities than we might, at first glance, think.

How good are we, then, as a species, at predicting how the future of common complex systems will unfold? This work hasn't been completed in training

TRAINING TALK

contexts but luckily there is an extensive literature reaching back over 60 years, testing expert predictive ability in other complex human endeavors.

MB: **What does that research say in terms of our predictive ability?**

KIELY: The most comprehensive and confidence shattering evidence was the mammoth 20-year study led by Phillip Tetlock. Tetlock was interested in testing human predictive ability, but this is no simple task. Typically, we have lots of ways of justifying our predictive errors, such as, "OK, I was wrong this time, but I was nearly right," or, "I would have been right if unexpected event 'X' didn't happen." So, the majority of the time, when we're "wrong," we either don't realize it, or we have convenient ways of excusing ourselves from being wrong. And, as a consequence, we frequently don't learn from past mistakes.

In other words, we rationalize events in ways that protect our egos. This is why upwards of 90% of college professors believe they are above average lecturers; 90% of drivers believe they are better than average drivers; and, the overwhelming majority of us believe we are more funny than nearly everyone else. Mathematically, none of this is possible, but it doesn't stop us believing it.

In Tetlock's study, the experts couldn't retrospectively adjust what they said to better match what eventually unfolded because they had to pre-commit to their predictions and justify how they came to their conclusions.

To cut a long story short, at the end of the study after more than 250 experts—all highly educated, highly experienced, and highly regarded thought leaders—had made over 10,000 predictions, the results were evaluated. The key conclusions, when I first read them, were like a bucket of ice water splashed over my cozy, snug and obviously delusional ego. The first conclusion was summarized neatly by Tetlock, "Expert predictions were about as accurate as dart-throwing chimps." In other words, expert predictions were no better than randomly generated guesses. As if that wasn't enough, there was an additional wrinkle: the experts who expressed the most confidence in their initial predictions were the least accurate, managing, somehow, to make the dart-throwing chimps look good.

Interestingly, during the study, the Soviet Union collapsed; from any angle, quite a notable event. After the dust settled, numerous commentators, with the benefit of hindsight, confidently explained how this was all but inevitable and how they, of course, had seen it coming. Yet, prior to the event, even though many experts specialized in foreign policy, none of them accurately predicted what was the single greatest social upheaval over the course of the 20-year study.

The final conclusion was a bit more subtle. During the study, Tetlock divided the experts into groups based on their decision-making styles. The first group were those who, when faced with a new situation, compared this situation to a previously encountered problem where they felt they had been successful. Then, they applied the same set of procedures and protocols to the new problem.

Essentially, they looked for similarities between previous and current problems, and then, re-applied historically successful solutions. As these experts persistently re-employed past strategies, Tetlock called these experts the "hedgehogs"—because hedgehogs repeatedly use one big trick to solve a broad range of problems.

The second group, in contrast, focused on the differences between past and current contexts. They considered each set of circumstances to be unique. Crucially, instead of comparing and seeking out similarities, they zoomed in on the differences between situations. These experts focused primarily on each situation's uniqueness and subsequently, evolved unique solutions to, what they perceived to be, unique problems. Tetlock termed this group the "foxes"—as foxes don't have one obvious survival trick, instead depending on a problem-solving agility to survive.

TRAINING TALK

So how did the experts fare? When the results of both groups were lumped together, predictive accuracy was universally poor—in itself, a stunning conclusion, considering how much faith we place in experts' predictive ability. When the groups were considered separately, there was a significant difference between each group's predictive accuracy, not huge, but significant.

The foxes consistently outperformed the hedgehogs. Why? Because, they treated each set of circumstances as inevitably unique and didn't simply mindlessly re-employ old solutions to current problems.

ELIMINATE IGNORANCE BY BANISHING ARROGANCE

MB: **Where does that leave us?**

KIELY: For me, conventional periodization dogma makes us all slightly more hedgehog-like. If we believe the woo-woo pseudo-science; if we believe the myth of a best periodization structure; if we think we've cracked the problem and have the solution; we've already closed our minds to the novelty of each situation. And we will be less alert; less observant; less agile in our training decision-making. As a consequence, our effectiveness will be diminished.

And, now that we are aware of the complexity of the problem and of the innate pitfalls of human psychology, we are faced with a choice. We can take the easy route and conform to a simplistic rule-based structure, but we can no longer legitimately justify this on the basis of periodization theory and its inherent assumptions of conformity and predictability.

The easy route is to be a planning hedgehog. Curl up around your favorite periodization model. Construct a storyline that supports, and persistently reinforces, your chosen beliefs. Believe in the biased interpretation of your experiences and favorable interpretations of your past actions. Grade yourself on a forgiving curve. Believe you have an innate gift denied to others.

Or take the hard road: be a fox. Embrace philosophical humility. Acknowledge you don't know the best solution. You can't predict the "best" training program in advance, and you certainly can't expect some off-the-shelf periodization model to do it for you. Accept that we don't know much about how the world works, and much of what we think we know is likely to be wrong. Stay observant and open-minded in the face of emerging information and don't fall into the traps afflicting those possessing an excessive sense of certainty and self-confidence.

>> *[T]ake the hard road; be a fox. Embrace philosophical humility. Acknowledge you don't know the best solution.*

We can't accurately predict how complex phenomena will unfold; we can't expect future results to conform to past results or the gains experienced by some, to be experienced by others. When we look back at the evolution of periodization theory, there hasn't been a lot of philosophical modesty on display. Unfortunately, periodization is also a heavily male-dominated domain. There's been a lot of, "I'm right; he's wrong," or, "My method's better; his is worse."

When I think of this, my mind always drifts to that sketch in Monty Python's *The Life of Brian*, the one where Brian's followers argue the significance of his lost shoe, all arriving at differing interpretations of the same simple observation, all utterly convinced of the legitimacy of their conclusions. If you haven't seen it, treat yourself to a smile and watch it.

So, strange as it seems, perhaps the most important thing we've learned is the extent of what we don't know. Even though it's uncomfortable, if we can embrace a philosophical humility in the face of complex and uncertain reality, I think, we will automatically be better planners, adapters and managers of the training process.

TRAINING TALK

MB: This reminds me of philosophy class and how the Oracle of Delphi pronounced Socrates the wisest of the Greeks because he knew that he did not know. But how do we move from eliminating ignorance to making sense of such complex phenomenon?

KIELY: We need to carefully weigh individual studies, personal experiences, practical observations and traditional beliefs against our conceptual model for understanding how the world, as it pertains to athletic preparation, really works. We need to arrive at conclusions based on an unbiased consideration of the spectrum of evidence. We need to put our egos to the side; we need to put our reverence of "experts" to the side; we need to put the security blanket of tradition to the side.

Coaching organizations and coach education systems typically tell us what to do rather than nurturing our understanding. We learn to parrot a series of hand-me-down rules, rather than deepening our appreciation of how complex phenomena really work. We learn what we should do to solve idealized problems instead of learning how to be problem-solvers.

> >> We learn what we should do to solve idealized problems, instead of learning how to be problem solvers.

The best coaches I know are critical thinkers: they may never have read an academic paper, but they test their assumptions and observe carefully. They are analytical, meticulous, diligent and self-reflective. And, because of this their belief systems are fluid, not carved in stone.

The ones I've least enjoyed working with are those who, because they already have all the answers, feel they don't need to strive every day. We expect athletes to commit, to work consistently to push their limits; we should hold ourselves to the same ideals.

FIVE QUESTIONS FOR COACHES TO CONSIDER

MB: **We started off by discussing the failings of modern periodization methods and you offered an alternative core philosophy based on the process rather than the plan. Good periodization, in your view, is about designing a good process. So then how to we take those general concepts and create a training plan?**

KIELY: I'm not a planning guru; I'm not pretending to be, and I'm not pretending to have a definitive answer. How can anyone have a definitive answer? But perhaps what I can offer is a series of questions. Questions, which, if adapted to our individual coaching contexts, might help us evolve a more insightful means of tackling the training management problem.

1. *What's your training philosophy?*

What do you believe? Why do you believe it? Because it's conventional? Because it's comfortable? Because it's been passed down in a path-dependent way? Or, because you have reflected deeply, and it best fits your current state of learning and experience?

Are your beliefs flexible? If not, why not? Because you are so certain of their truth that you refuse to consider they may be in error? Because you are emotionally attached to them? Because you have invested so much in them that even contemplating change is too uncomfortable?

If your beliefs are either set in stone or change in response to fads and fashion, gimmicks or shiny toys, maybe you need to review the threshold of evidence necessary to motivate you to realign your philosophy. Is your skepticism level set too high for arguments which contradict your favored beliefs and too low for propositions you want to believe in? If so, welcome to the club! We're all human; we all have these embedded tendencies. But, once we are aware of the problem, our duty—if we wish to be clearer thinkers—is to reset our inner detective so we make decisions based on careful unbiased reflection; not on emotional knee-jerk responses.

TRAINING TALK

Your underlying philosophy steers all training designs and decisions. It should be a fusion of all your experiences and learning. If you want it to be robust, you need to invest time and energy; you need to evolve it.

2. *What's your planning structure?*
Have a plan. Put a shape on it. We all need a map, a destination to zoom in on. Athletes need to know where, when, how long, how frequent, and roughly how hard. But, what's your planning horizon? How far in advance do you need to plan, and to what level of detail?

When will you sit, review progress and plan forward? How often? With who? What data—opinions, perspectives, training records, medical information, competition dates—will help inform that session?

Do you advance plan the what-ifs, the if this, then that scenarios? In other words: do you plan to change your plan?

Do you having a planning checklist? A list of all the things you need to do to make your process as efficient and effective as possible? What questions do you ask the athletes before every session? Are they consistent? Are you sure? We're human; we forget; we assume; we overlook. Don't leave the silly little stuff to chance; make sure it's nailed on. Build checklists; build routines. If you try and remember everything, you will be a hostage to your fallible human memory, and you will make more errors than you should.

>> *It's not about being perfect; it's about being better.*

The adaptive response to future training is inherently unpredictable. Hence, advance planning of training demands wiggle room, a certain level of leeway. But, other dimensions of the training process can be rigorously planned. Yes, it's mostly the boring logistical stuff, but boring logistical stuff needs doing! Don't be a coach who is a great theorist, but always late, always forgetting kit, never organized. But don't be a hyper-organized slave to the rigidity of the spreadsheet. As always, the very best gracefully walk the middle path. For the rest of us, it's an ongoing tug-of-war. It's not about being perfect; it's about being better.

3. *What's your strategy for optimizing athlete belief in the program?*
You might have the best, most scientifically-validated and most carefully considered training plan in the history of sport. But, if your athletes don't believe in it, they won't fully commit and they won't fully benefit. I may have a mediocre, run-of-the-mill program, but if the athletes have faith—if the athletes make a direct connection between the training I ask them to do today and the fulfilment of their sporting dreams—then these athletes are more likely to thrive.

Why? If I believe a particular training organization will work for me, then it is automatically more likely to do so. I confidently commit. I don't stress about my direction forward. Whereas, if I don't fully believe, I am a little hesitant. Perhaps I worry more than I should. Perhaps, as a result, I don't sleep so well. When the pressure is on, doubt bubbles to the surface like a body rising in a bog. And suddenly, through a hundred different avenues, the effectiveness of my overall training process is diminished.

So, Martin, when you were training with Bondarchuk, for example, one of the things he brings to the table is that he practically owns hammer throwing. You have faith. It is like the placebo effect in medicine. More accurately, it's an "expectancy effect." You get better because you expect to get better, and it's a very real thing.

Importantly, coaches shouldn't just demand that the athlete has faith. A deep faith in the program can only be earned. Irrevocably linked to this deep faith, is the athletes sense of ownership, a sense that they have contributed to the program and that their voice, expressing their thoughts and concerns, is heard and respected.

TRAINING TALK

The scale of this contribution is tied to something we rarely talk about in coaching circles: how we educate athletes, how we nurture the athletes understanding of the training process. Do we educate them? Should we? What kind of conversations should we be having with athletes aged 20 versus 25 versus 30?

Too often, we see mature athletes changing camp, for whatever reason, and despite having a good training age, they are unable to provide meaningful opinions on what training interventions may or may not work for them. Why? Because previous coaches never involved them in decision-making; never involved them in training conversations; never gave them a platform to air their thoughts. Instead, training was dictated to them; their perspectives weren't sought; their opinions weren't respected; their intellectual growth was stunted. As a consequence, you end up with senior athletes unable to have meaningfully insightful conversations. Because of this, the individuals with the most vitally important feedback information don't fully understand what it means and can't accurately convey it to their coaches.

From poor communication comes poor decisions, and we make mistakes. We undertrain, we overtrain, and we injure. So, how do you develop your athlete's insight? Do you nurture their understanding? Do you educate? Are you a dictator or a collaborator?

4. *What's your training prescription strategy?*
One of the great myths of periodization is that conforming to the numbers, in terms of sets and reps, guarantees the desired training effect. But, your brain and biology don't see the numbers; they respond only to sensations and intensities. The adaptive response is regulated NOT by the imposed training stress, but by the combination of training stress overlaid on the current state of the athlete's system, which itself is constantly shifting.

And so, the relationship between sets, reps, mileage and so on and the adaptive response is much more indirect than we are traditionally led to believe. Adding a further element of confusion: training prescribed is rarely training performed.

> >> *Training prescribed is rarely training performed.*

Interestingly, in the past, when researchers compared coach prescription against training execution, they found substantial discrepancies, especially in relation to intensities of completed training. And, these discrepancies were not due to the athlete purposefully disobeying instructions. The athletes thought they were working at the effort levels coaches prescribed. Instead, training errors were due to lack of clarity and poorly defined intensity levels. In other words, poor communication.

Today, thanks to the ever-accelerating technological revolution, there are many ways to numerically control training—instrumented cranks, GPS, accelerometers, and so on. Undoubtedly these are incredibly useful tools. But, do we run a risk, if we fixate on the numbers, of detracting from our focus on quality of technical execution and subjective feel?

So, should we prescribe in sets and reps? Should we monitor and record only the empirical descriptors of training performed? Or should we seek to integrate more execution quality parameters and subjective feel into both our instructions and our training records?

In your training context, can you meaningfully enhance your prescriptive accuracy by better triangulating between the numerical descriptors of training, athlete interpretation of intensity, and execution quality?

5. *What's your process for capturing information?*
When will you pause, review and redirect? What data do you need to optimally inform this review? Are you capturing that information now?

TRAINING TALK

Of course, the data you collect will depend on many factors: the sport, the level, contact time with the athletes, the degree to which key dimensions of the sport are readily quantifiable.

We're living in the era of Big Data. So many new tools, devices and apps enabling us to collect so many previously unavailable streams of information, but how do we use them? How do we interpret them? We're flooded with interesting snapshots, but what do they mean?

A very real danger of Big Data may be that it distracts our attention from critical information by burying it under mounds of potentially interesting, but non-vital stats. Ultimately, a wealth of information is useless if it leads to a poverty of insight.

> *>> Ultimately, a wealth of information is useless if it leads to a poverty of insight.*

We think of training data as numbers, but data can also take the form of observations, notes, opinions, and perceptions. But, how do you collect those? Do you think you will remember them all when it comes to review? If your memory is that good, rest assured you are more gifted than the overwhelming majority of us because human memory is a notoriously myopic distortion device. I don't trust mine, and so some of the first items in my work bag are always a notebook and pen.

I'm all for new technology: it provides previously unavailable information enabling better insight, better tracking, better learning experiences. But, it doesn't replace observation; it only complements it.

So, for me at least, data collection isn't just about collecting numbers and whatever they may represent. It's also about documenting observations and thoughts and new ideas and suggestions. Sometimes we have flashes of inspiration, triggered by just watching and thinking. I don't get enough of flashes of inspiration, so when they do occur, I desperately need to capture them.

> \>\> *I'm all for new technology, but it doesn't replace observation, it only complements it.*

FINAL COMMENT

MB: **What are your parting words for coaches on planning?**

KIELY: Nobel Prize winning psychologist, Daniel Kahneman, once wrote, "We have an almost unlimited ability to ignore our ignorance." In the case of training planning, acknowledging our ignorance may be our redemption. When you're planning, it pays to be a bit paranoid. Don't trust the consenting voices in your head; don't trust the secondhand information of experts. Work through it. Figure it out. Decide on your first step. Then, temporarily, park it. Execute. Record. Review. Refine. Redirect. It is not easy. If we pretend it is easy and accept old mechanical periodization logic, then, we will make more mistakes and more errors of judgement than we should.

Accept that it's a complex balancing act. You need structure, but not something too rigid. You need adaptive flexibility, but it can't be too loose. You need consistency, but monotony is dangerous. Change is a potent adaptive stimulus, but sudden change is recklessly dangerous. Sorry. There's no black and white, only shades of grey.

I'm back room staff, and the nature of my work is that—depending on the contract and the context—sometimes I plan, but more frequently I work within somebody else's plan. In situations where I'm operating within the constraints of an already formulated periodized program, I'm rarely excessively concerned with the actual structure of the plan, most are logi-

TRAINING TALK

cal and reasonable. I am, however, far more interested in the design of the "process." How does the manager/coach make informed decisions, collect opinions and information, communicate the plan to athletes, and ensure athletes understand and fully buy into the plan. Do they pay attention to context? Do they think deeply, or are they on automatic pilot? Are they taking steps to design a learning process, or do they feel they already know? Are they looking for sycophantic followers to agree, or devil's advocates to respectfully challenge?

I most admire those who are fox-like, who balance structured consistency with a readiness to trim and adapt—those who observe closely, pay attention to detail, who seek to challenge their most cherished beliefs, coaches who are humble in the face of success and resilient in the face of failure. Who, if they're successful, don't start to believe they're omnipotent; and if they're unsuccessful don't lose faith in their process.

Success, as counted by major championships and medals, is dependent on so much more than training planning. You, for example, may manage training brilliantly, but because you don't have access to a funnel of talent, you don't get the accolades. I, on the other hand, am an inferior planner and process-designer, but because I was in the right place when opportunity came knocking—in the form of a superior genetic specimen—I go on to success; I go on the lecture tours; I write the books; I become the "expert." Don't get me wrong, I'm not suggesting its all luck, of course it's not: far from it. But the random alignment of circumstances plays a part.

And so, the distinction between excellent and poor training management is not clear-cut. We operate in environments where excellence often goes unnoticed, and poor practice often persists. The need for change is not immediately apparent; hence, change emerges slowly.

Our conventional perspectives, periodization mythology, distracting anecdotes of how legendary athletes trained, are not worthless, but they are feeble validations of a training philosophy. We can't trust them, and they need to be appropriately weighted.

I feel as if I've short-changed your readers. I've rabbited on about periodization, and I've not once mentioned the term "macro-cycle" or suggested the ideal number of weeks for a training phase. I haven't even made up a new name for this type of periodization. I really am a rubbish periodization theorist! But, I hope it's provided some food for thought.

And finally . . . We all like a good quote, and I'll finish with this one by the excellent surgeon and writer Atul Gawande. It nicely captures my key concluding sentiment more eloquently than I ever could:

> Better is possible. It does not take genius. It takes diligence. It takes moral clarity. It takes ingenuity. Above all, it takes a willingness to try.

We can all be better planners. We just need to more clearly understand the nature of the problem. Then, we need to bend our work processes and thinking styles around this reality. Not simply by collecting experiences, but by subjecting our experiences—our successes and failures—to careful, unbiased scrutiny. If we fail to do this, we are not really learning, we are just clocking up time.

Once we better understand the nature of the problem, once we acknowledge the confounding influence of our egos, our embedded biases, our deep-seated human tendencies to rationalize events in ways buffering self-confidence and deflecting self-critique, then, our vision clears. And, we see that the way forward lies not in regurgitating old comforting periodization shortcuts, but in breaking out of the path-dependent planning ruts so deeply embedded in our training cultures.

Then, I believe we can, with a head cleared of mythological debris, crack on with the business of customizing our planning processes to best fit our specific training contexts.

AFTERWORD

HUMANS HAVE AN uncanny ability to find what they're looking for. Or, to put it more accurately, humans have an uncanny ability to think they've found what they're looking for, whether it's there or not. In the world of psychology and behavioral economics this is called confirmation bias. Simply put, we all have a tendency to search for, interpret, favor, and recall information in a way that confirms our own beliefs.

One great example of this comes from wide-ranging research at Stanford University. In one of their studies, opponents and proponents of capital punishment were presented with fictional research papers on the topic. When asked to evaluate the same body of work, participants consistently pointed to details that supported their viewpoint and disregarding anything contrary. This latter point, setting higher standards for evidence contrary to your opinions, even has its own name: disconfirmation bias.

Hopefully you've learned something from all the discussions in this book, and if not at least it was food for thought. As you start to reflect on what you've seen and learned in the preceding pages, keep confirmation bias in mind.

In line with this I'm willing to bet that the most common reaction to this book will be to cite it as evidence for how your existing coaching methods

TRAINING TALK

are correct. I say this because it was my initial reaction after each interview. The danger as an interviewer is that confirmation bias is everywhere. You select the coaches, define the subjects, and guide the conversation. Whether you want to or not, you start to identify with things you already agree with. The people, the subjects, and the questions all tend not to stray too far from what you think is the right way to train and coach.

The reader cannot control the narrative, but they are not immune to biases either. You picked up this book for a reason, and the same issues arise.

I tried to step outside this, but bias can never be fully avoided. The best one can do is be aware of the bias and slow down to think a little more. Nobel prize winner Daniel Kahnemann and his colleague Amos Tversky spent their careers outlining cognitive bias, and this is one of their suggestions too. It will help you think twice about what you read and whether it actually supports what you do.

Another trick is to consciously try to think about the differences, rather than the similarities, that the coaches present. This is an exercise in critical thinking. It might seem ironic that I'm writing about the importance of differences after spending the whole introduction discussing the importance of similarities. But looking at the differences is the natural progression after looking at similarities.

Similarities are still of the utmost importance. If every elite coach is doing something, it is worth investigating that a bit further. In the introduction I highlighted some of these similarities, and each one is crucial for every coach to know. The similarities make up the foundation of coaching. But the art of coaching lies in the differences.

Thinking about differences is also something John Kiely mentioned when reviewing Philip Tetlock's work on prediction. The group Tetlock called hedgehogs trailed the foxes when it came to predictions. One major difference between the two groups is that hedgehogs looked for similarities

Afterword

when making predictions, whiles foxes looked at the differences. The importance of differences goes far beyond the world of predictions.

Differences can challenge our beliefs in many cases, but at a smaller level they also help us understand nuance. If two coaches have the same core philosophy but implement different plans, understanding the differences helps us understand why that is. Perhaps they are addressing needs of different athletes, or interpreting feedback differently. By asking why, rather than what, we learn more. By focusing on the process, not just the plan, we find the nuance.

To take coaching to the next level, be the fox. Make the effort, ask the difficult questions, and challenge yourself. If there is one lesson you take from the book, I hope that is it.

ACKNOWLEDGEMENTS

ONLY BY SHARING can we all grow so thanks goes first and foremost to the dozen coaches who shared their time and ideas making this book possible.

This book is the culmination of a life-long journey to learn more about coaching. The desire to learn was instilled in me by my first two mentors, the late Harold Connolly and Anatoliy Bondarchuk. Despite reaching the top of their sport, they showed me you can never stop learning.

Vern Gambetta has been crucial in opening up his network to me, connecting me with many of the authors in this book. Both he and Nick Garcia set aside an hour a week to produce our podcasts, and both keep me on my toes and seeing training from a new perspective.

There are hundreds of steps between an idea and a finished product, and my family has been essential to taking each step. My wife, sister-in-law Greta Wesslen, and my parents all devoted countless hours to editing various drafts. My daughter Reese also helped by taking long naps so we could squeeze the work in.

ABOUT THE AUTHOR

G. Martin Bingisser is a Swiss-American coach. He is currently the Swiss national hammer throw coach, as well as the hammer throwing coach for Leichtathletik-Club Zürich and fitness coach for GC Rugby Zürich. His athletes have captured more than 20 national titles.

Born and raised in Seattle, Washington, Bingisser attended the University of Washington. He spent nearly a decade training under the guidance of former Soviet national coach Anatoliy Bondarchuk, and throughout his career has won two NCAA All-American honors, eight Swiss national titles, and competed at the 2014 European Championships.

Bingisser is also active in coaches education. As founder of HMMR Media and the non-profit Evergreen Athletic Fund, he has consulted on coaching and continuing education for athletics federations (European Athletics, USATF, UK Athletics, Swiss Athletics, Scottish Athletics and Belgian Athletics) and professional rugby clubs (English Rugby, Scottish Rugby, Munster Rugby, and Northampton Saints). He is also a GAIN faculty member.

His first book, *The Ball and Chain: A Guide to Hammer Throwing*, was published in 2015. He has also published articles in leading print and online publications, and co-hosts both the HMMR Podcast and GAINcast.

CPSIA information can be obtained
at www.ICGtesting.com
Printed in the USA
FSHW010016210619
59181FS